Morality and Foreign Policy
Realpolitik Revisited

Kenneth M. Jensen and Elizabeth P. Faulkner
Editors

UNITED STATES
INSTITUTE OF PEACE

Washington, D.C.

The views expressed in this book are those of the authors alone. They do not necessarily reflect views of the United States Institute of Peace.

United States Institute of Peace
1550 M Street, N.W.
Washington, D.C. 20005

First published 1991

Printed in the United States of America

The paper used in this publication meets the minimum requirements of American National Standard for Information Sciences—Permanence of Paper for Printed Library Materials, ANSI Z39.48-1984.

Library of Congress Cataloging-in-Publication Data
Morality and foreign policy: realpolitik revisited / Kenneth M. Jensen
and Elizabeth P. Faulkner, editors.
   p. cm.
Based on the Morality and Foreign Policy Public Workshop, held in Atlanta, Ga., in spring 1989, and cosponsored by the United States Institute of Peace and the Carter Center, Emory University.
Includes bibliographical references.
   ISBN 1-878379-09-7 (pbk.)
   1. United States—Foreign relations—1945—Moral and ethical aspects—Congresses. 2. International relations—Moral and ethical aspects—Congresses. 3. Kennan, George Frost, 1904- —Views on foreign relations—Congresses. 4. National Security—Moral and ethical aspects—Congresses. I. Jensen, Kenneth M. (Kenneth Martin), 1944- . II. Faulkner, Elizabeth P. III. Morality and Foreign Policy Public Workshop (1989 : Atlanta, Ga.) IV. United States Institute of Peace. V. Emory University. Carter Center.
JX1417.M68 1991   90-25576
172'.4—dc20   CIP

United States Institute of Peace

The United States Institute of Peace is an independent, nonpartisan, federal institution created and wholly funded by Congress to strengthen the nation's capacity to promote the peaceful resolution of international conflict. Established in 1984, the Institute has its origins in the tradition of American statesmanship, which seeks to limit international violence and to achieve a just peace based on freedom and human dignity. The Institute meets its congressional mandate to expand available knowledge about ways to achieve a more peaceful world through an array of programs including grantmaking, a three-tiered fellowship program, research and studies projects, development of library resources, and a variety of citizen education activities. The Institute is governed by a bipartisan, fifteen-member Board of Directors, including four ex officio members from the executive branch of the federal government and eleven individuals appointed from outside federal service by the President of the United States and confirmed by the Senate.

Board of Directors

Other publications in the Dialogues from Public Workshops series:

A Discussion of the Origins of Thinking on Arms Control: The Sarajevo Fallacy

The Meaning of Munich Fifty Years Later

A Look at "The End of History?"

Is It Feasible to Negotiate Chemical and Biological Weapons Control?

Pacifism and Citizenship: Can They Coexist?

Other recent publications from the United States Institute of Peace:

Approaches to Peace: An Intellectual Map

Guides to Library of Congress Subject Headings and Classification on Peace and International Conflict Resolution

Negotiating Across Cultures: Communication Obstacles in International Diplomacy

Origins of the Cold War: The Novikov, Kennan, and Roberts Long Telegrams of 1946

Soviet-American Conflict Resolution in the Third World

Ukraine: The Legacy of Intolerance

Contents

Preface

Is there an ethical vacuum in Washington? This subject, raised at a spring 1989 public workshop in Atlanta, Georgia, cosponsored by the United States Institute of Peace and the Carter Center of Emory University, was frankly meant to be provocative. The panel on Morality and Foreign Policy was asked to consider the moral implications of three decisions, each of which had adversely affected U.S. friends abroad.

In the 1950s, the panel was reminded, American politicians and the Voice of America encouraged Eastern Europeans to "roll back the Iron Curtain." But when the Hungarians rose against their Communist regime, the U.S. administration, fearful of starting World War III, watched the rebellion die under the tracks of Soviet tanks. Two decades later, the United States and Iran encouraged another popular uprising by covertly pouring arms and money into the Kurdish brushfire war against Iraq. This policy lasted until the Shah of Iran decided to mend his fences with Baghdad. Washington promptly abandoned the Kurdish independence struggle. More recently American foreign policymakers downplayed the malevolent Syrian role in the mayhem in Lebanon, a friendly Arab country, on the grounds that it did not pose a "direct threat" to U.S. security. What, the panel was asked, did these decisions say about the moral content of U.S. foreign policy?

Somewhat surprisingly, the scholars, human rights advocates, and foreign policy experts participating in the workshop responded with little more than an exasperated shrug of their shoulders. However, Dayle E. Powell, director of the Conflict Resolution Program at the Carter Center, faulted Washington for leaving "complex moral analysis" out of its decision making. Washington seems to operate on the assumption that "the world is our chessboard," and most foreign countries are "pawns in a larger game," she complained.

Lack of animation about this question did not carry over to the rest of the discussion. The workshop, in fact, overflowed with indignation—but its primary target was the intellectual architect of U.S. foreign policy after World War II. Former career diplomat George Kennan has been widely praised for articulating the containment strategy that checked the spread of Stalinism in the 1950s. However, according to David Little, a former Institute distinguished fellow and now its senior scholar, Kennan concurrently persuaded the American foreign policy establishment that ethics play no proper role in national security considerations. Kennan's hardnosed realpolitik is even now "enormously influential" in Washington, Little told the workshop.

Giving an example of what he sees as Kennan's amoral guidelines, Little quoted from a 1947 policy paper in which Kennan argued that huge economic and political disparities between the United States and much of postwar Asia were unavoidable. "We should stop putting ourselves in the position of being our brother's keeper and refrain from offering moral and ideological advice," Kennan wrote. "We should cease to talk about vague and—for the Far East—unreal objectives such as human rights, the raising of living standards, and democratization. The day is not far off when we are going to have to deal in straight power concepts. The less we are hampered by idealistic slogans, the better off we are."

The Japanese success story—not only economic but political—and recent calls for democracy in other Asian countries demonstrate the fallacy of Kennan's belief that American values would not flourish elsewhere, Little maintained. In his view, Kennan also failed to recognize that the American dedication to democratic principles lends U.S. security interests an inseparable moral dimension. "The heart of Kennan's problem," Little charged, was his overemphasis on the so-called "necessity defense," a time-honored but rarely applied principle that places survival above ethical considerations. "For George Kennan, international relations are really nothing but a long dismal series of 'necessity' situations," in which morality goes by the wayside, Little summed up.

Kennan's sole defender on the panel, Professor Theodore Weber from the theological faculty at Emory, vigorously denied that he was a "consistent political amoralist." Kennan spoke "mainly about the ends of foreign policy, not the means," but he would react with a "great deal of outrage" to behavior unbecoming a democracy, Weber insisted. The reason Kennan wanted U.S. foreign policy to "proceed in terms of power relations and national interests and not in terms of democratization and human rights," Weber held, was his conviction that any other course would be rejected by other nations and peoples. According to Weber, Kennan regarded as "presumptuous" Americans' trying to tell other societies, of which they know little, that democracy is best for them; moreover, he believed that these societies would distrust the U.S. motives. "They would say, 'Oh come on, [the Americans] can't really mean [their enthusiasm for democracy]. The U.S. must be carving out its spheres of influence, and this is just window dressing,'" Weber paraphrased Kennan's arguments.

But Kennan's critics were not mollified. A severe critic of the purported U.S. penchant for realpolitik was Richard Joseph, a fellow at the Carter Center and director of its Governance in Africa Program. Locked in the cold war, the United States automatically opposed Third World governments that were supported by the Soviet Union, Joseph charged. The strategy was the apex of the "nonethical approach of foreign policy" and, in Joseph's view, was "highly destructive to the emerging African nations." Yet when it suited vested American interests, Joseph complained, Washington could urge other countries to elect a "morally based" government, as it did not long ago in Panama. "We are very selective about it," Joseph said. The Noriega regime, he added, was "not the only one which has been involved in drugs and falsified elections," but the others have not come under U.S. pressure.

Former Sudanese Foreign Minister Francis Deng, a senior fellow at the Brookings Institution and, at the time of the workshop, a distinguished fellow at the United States Institute of Peace, countered the claim—which Little had attributed to Kennan—that nations do not share the same moral values. Using several folktales and other anecdotes from the Dinka culture, Deng asserted that while each society has particular "values around which it structures its social relationships and the whole purpose of life," all recognize the same fundamental principles of human dignity. These principles may be expressed in a variety of disparate ways and may be realized in varying degrees, but they are universal. He went on to tell a story about trying to get his editors to understand that his use of the word *gentleman* in describing a Dinka with certain values was not merely an attempt to make him seem like an Englishman. To Deng's mind, the word expressed human values that transcend culture.

Kennan's injunctions have been eroding for some time, according to Powell. The debate over whether U.S. advocacy of human rights is good foreign policy "has been won," she pointed out, and—at least with respect to the Soviet Union—defense of humanitarian concerns has been "an area of continuity" between the administrations of Jimmy Carter and Ronald Reagan. Powell suggested two reasons for the evolution of the new moral environment. One was an "equal necessity" for peace that has been imposed on all nations, big and small, by the atomic age. The fact that "humanity can no

longer accept the existence of war as preordained," Powell
suggested, has spurred such nonviolent approaches to conflict resolution as the Aquino revolution in the Philippines
and the Solidarity movement in Poland.

The other key element in the new climate, in Powell's
analysis, is the U.S. defense of human rights everywhere,
which placed new responsibility on the executive. "Jimmy
Carter . . . had the view that the U.S. president was not in
office to simply serve the needs of U.S. citizens," but was also
duty-bound to "compare U.S. interests with [the] interests of
other countries," Powell argued. Since then, she said, "the
human rights discussion has really begun to alter the [tradi-
tional] moral equation" in international affairs. Weber
summed up the evolving American ethos in similar terms.
The U.S. president, he said, "has moral responsibility to look
after [American] interests, but that's not the whole of it. At a
minimum, there are responsibilities to those who are affected
by our exercise of power. To decide that our own people have
more value than others—that is a religious decision."

Changing expectations in the U.S. policy-making community have been accompanied by unsettling questions. For
instance, one of the participants asked, would the East-West
thaw wipe out American foreign aid to Third World
countries, which Congress has traditionally authorized as a
defense against communism? Whatever the future brings,
the panel agreed, the answers are not to be found in the old
arsenal of postwar policy. "Kennan reflected his era, which
was dominated by the cold war," Joseph concluded. "We are
entering a new era, and we need new Kennans."

The political transformations that have occurred in
Eastern Europe and the Soviet Union in the past few years
do, indeed, call for a reevaluation of the relationship between
morality and U.S. foreign policy. The cold war landscape that
Kennan surveyed is now almost unrecognizable, and his
caution against America's talking to other nations about such
"vague" objectives as "human rights, the raising of living
standards, and democratization" no longer seems

appropriate. As the number of democratic nations grows, so too does the likelihood that foreign policies will be expected to display ethical as well as realpolitik considerations. In short, the issues raised at this public workshop have never been more relevant than today.

This publication contains the text of the discussion at the Morality and Foreign Policy Public Workshop. It begins with David Little's extended remarks on the question; continues with commentary by Francis Deng, Theodore Weber, Richard Joseph, and Dayle E. Powell; and then moves to a general discussion. Included as an appendix is a pertinent article by George F. Kennan, "Morality and Foreign Policy," which first appeared in *Foreign Affairs* in its Winter 1985/86 issue.

The Institute is especially grateful to the staff of the Carter Center for hosting the event and for making important contributions to this lively debate about the proper place of moral considerations in American statecraft.

Samuel W. Lewis, President
United States Institute of Peace

DAVID LITTLE

Morality and National Security

No one has put the problem of relating morality and national security so provocatively as George F. Kennan, that venerable scholar-diplomat and Soviet expert. I single out George Kennan because I believe he has been and continues to be enormously influential in regard to this subject. Whenever I discuss the topic of morality and national security with diplomats or government officials, as I do on occasion, I am struck again and again by how much Kennan's thought informs many of the attitudes present in those discussions.

There are, of course, people such as Reinhold Niebuhr and Hans Morgenthau who have in some way shared Kennan's approach to international affairs. However, I believe that Kennan's influence on the practice of diplomacy has been greater than theirs. Possibly because Kennan was himself a diplomat, he has been taken very seriously by the foreign policy community. My second reason for singling out Kennan is that he is currently experiencing something of a renaissance. He frequently appears on television and has just issued a new book, *Sketches From a Life*, in which he recounts his experience in the Foreign Service.[1]

For reasons very much inspired by his diplomatic experience, Kennan believes that we should, in effect, dissociate or disjoin the ideas of morality from national security and national self-interest. Upon becoming the first director

1

of the State Department's Policy Planning Staff just after World War II, he laid out in a classified memorandum the following long-range design for U.S. foreign policy toward Asia:

> [W]e have about 50 percent of the world's wealth but only 6.3 percent of its population. This disparity is particularly great as between ourselves and the peoples of Asia. In this situation, we cannot fail to be the object of envy and resentment. Our real task in the coming period is to devise a pattern of relationships which will permit us to maintain this position of disparity without positive detriment to our national security. To do so, we will have to dispense with all sentimentality and day-dreaming—.
>
> We should dispense with the aspiration to "be liked" or to be regarded as the repository of a high-minded international altruism. We should stop putting ourselves in the position of being our brother's keeper and refrain from offering moral and ideological advice. We should cease to talk about vague and—for the Far East—unreal objectives such as human rights, the raising of living standards, and democratization. The day is not far off when we are going to have to deal in straight power concepts. The less we are hampered by idealistic slogans, the better.[2]

The bifurcation between morality and the pursuit of national security is a pervasive theme throughout Kennan's writings.[3] He asserts that morality must be detached from the purposes and functions of government because morality is a thoroughly relative matter, which cannot provide a basis for peace and security among nations:

> [L]et us not assume that our moral values, based as they are on the specifics of our national tradition and the various religious outlooks represented in our country, necessarily have validity for people everywhere. In particular, let us not assume that the purposes of states—are fit subjects for measurement in moral terms.[4]

Even more explicitly, Kennan wrote in the Winter 1985/86 issue of *Foreign Affairs* (in an article reprinted in the appendix to this volume) that the fundamental concerns of government, namely, the protection of its people, have no moral quality.[5] He acknowledges that governments will have to respond to the moral and other concerns of their citizens. However, such a response is a completely open-ended affair, subject to the vagaries and fluctuations of public opinion. There is no reason, he writes, to believe that morality can serve "as a general criterion for the determination of the behavior of states and above all as a criterion for measuring and comparing the behavior of different states. . . . Here other criteria, sadder, more limited, more practical, must be allowed to prevail."[6]

According to Kennan, morality—understood here as a commitment to protecting human rights, raising living standards, and democratization—is in the realm of subjective aspiration, a realm that varies to some extent from individual to individual, and to a great extent from society to society. The moral claims of one culture are inevitably doubted by another; there is nothing universal about such claims.

In contrast to morality, national security—the "interest" of every nation in self-preservation—is in the realm of "need," of "necessity," and is therefore something shared universally by all people. As such, the imperative of national security constitutes a common, practical (if limited) ground for mutual understanding and collaboration, whereas morality, because it varies among societies and cultures, does not. To confuse the two realms does more harm than good: in the words of the ancient Latin adage, *In necessariis unitas; in dubiis libertas* ("In necessities, unity; in doubts, liberty"). In short, national sovereignty and self-preservation become the basis on which realistic and pragmatic relations can take place, providing—according to Kennan—the only reliable foundation for international peace.[7]

Defining Terms

When evaluating Kennan's position, it is essential to examine carefully his understanding of the terms *national security* and *morality*. Does he accurately define and describe them? Do his definitions actually apply to real-world situations?

To begin, Kennan has a disconcertingly fixed view of national security. It is true that groups of people, including nations, are committed to their own preservation. Indeed, much of the collective life of a nation is shaped and organized around securing itself, by means of military defense and economic strength, against external and internal threats. It is also true that widespread violent assaults against a nation, dire natural catastrophes, or severe economic dislocation constitute a "clear and present danger" to a nation's security. Such events inevitably focus national attention and call for a concerted and urgent response.

But these truisms do not illuminate the meaning of the concept of national security very much. Nations obviously do not wait passively for armed attacks or uprisings to occur before reacting. They must anticipate; they must calculate the probabilities of military or other threats and take precautionary measures. It is here that complications arise: deciding which policies will actually achieve military security, deciding, for example, whether to focus on the Strategic Defense Initiative or to fund the Nicaraguan resistance.

Take, for example, the experience of the Iran-*contra* scandal during the latter part of the Reagan administration; it is clear from that example that perceptions of external and internal threats can vary sharply. In his account of the scandal, Bob Woodward reports that after President Reagan was shot in March 1981, "The Reagan presidency, from the inside, would never be the same. That sense of peril, that anyone or anything might strike—terrorists, a quick move from the Soviets, other adversaries—became a permanent, ingrained maxim of Administration policy."[8]

The attempted assassination of Reagan intensified CIA Director William Casey's concern with a worldwide, Soviet-dominated terrorist conspiracy, such as Claire Sterling alleged existed in *The Terror Network*.[9] Casey was convinced by Sterling's theory that the most severe threats to U.S. national security were posed by the Libyans, the Palestinian Liberation Organization, the Sandinistas, and others whose efforts were centrally coordinated and directed by the Soviets.

Casey's intelligence officers did not agree. Evidence did not support the theory. "The covert operators argued," writes Woodward, "that Sterling's method was preposterous. Her verdict followed from flawed reasoning—a kind of McCarthyist 'linkmanship.' Similarly, having sifted through all the available material, the national-intelligence officer for the Soviet Union 'took a strong anti-Sterling line.' But such massive disagreement had little effect on Casey. 'Read Claire Sterling's book and forget this mush,' he told them."[10] The conflicting perceptions of threat to national security continued throughout Casey's six-year tenure as director. Three distinguished deputies, Robert Inman, John Horton, and John McMahon, eventually resigned from the agency because they deeply disagreed with Casey's reading of the world. There was no easy consensus on national security.

There are additional difficulties with assuming that national security is something clear-cut. Not all threats to national security simply imperil physical safety. Danger to the fabric of economic life can also be a matter of national security, and thus there is room for conflicting opinion about the shape and source of such a danger, just as there is regarding military threats. Current debates among politicians over "economic-security issues" exemplify this point.

Richard Ullman defines danger to national security as any "action or sequence of events that (1) threatens drastically and over a relatively brief span of time to degrade the quality of life for the inhabitants of a state, or (2) threatens significantly to narrow the range of policy choices available to the government of a state or to private, nongovernmental entities—within the state."[11]

With this definition, the opportunities for conflicting judgments and estimates increase even more. Although the United States, as a nation, may come to some rough agreement as to what minimally constitutes an intolerable degradation of its common life and an unacceptable narrowing of public and private choices, it is easy to imagine a considerable range of disagreement and dispute beyond that bare minimum.

National security rests on complicated judgments and evaluations; it is, as philosophers would say, a normatively laden term. Consequently, it is subject to the variety of interpretations that inevitably accompany making involved evaluations, assessments, and judgments.

This point is particularly clear when it is recalled that a notion such as "the quality of life of the inhabitants of a state" includes not only military and economic matters but also a nation's ideals—out-and-out questions of moral commitment and loyalty. These, too, must be figured into any fair accounting of national security. A nation like the United States cares about and undertakes to defend not only its sheer physical and economic security, but its distinctive institutions: constitutional government; civil and political freedoms, including rights to equal treatment, free conscience, political participation, free expression, and legal protection; and a whole range of other democratic institutions. These things, these moral commitments, are part of what must be secured "against all enemies, foreign and domestic." They are part of national security.

In short, Harold Lasswell and Abraham Kaplan put it accurately, if somewhat clumsily, when they defined security as "high value expectancy": to be secure is to have confidence that one's "valuables" are there to be enjoyed.[12] A nation's security consists in the assurance that *all* its "national valuables" are protected.

Only for Americans?

So far, two problems with Kennan's approach are evident. First, the concept of national security does not correspond to anything very tidy or fixed, as Kennan's description would suggest. In fact, the term is rather porous. Deciding what constitutes national security requires very complicated calculations; it requires trying to harmonize the imperatives of physical security with the imperatives of economic and institutional (or "moral") security. In addition, it requires the determination of actual threats to these valuables, the relative severity of the different threats, and how to respond to them without unnecessarily compromising other valuables.

Second, a special problem for Kennan is posed by the fact that the ideals and commitments underlying civic institutions are an indispensable part of the national valuables and, as such, are a proper security concern. Consequently, we may be skeptical of Kennan's sharp distinction between morality and national security.

There is further reason to resist Kennan's formulation. American moral commitments, traditionally understood, apply not only to citizens of the United States, but universally: "all men [or, as we now say, human beings] are created equal;—are endowed by their Creator with certain unalienable rights—" according to Thomas Jefferson in the Declaration of Independence.

The beliefs that underlie the federal Constitution and the Declaration of Independence, as well as certain colonial state constitutions and early formative documents, such as the Virginia Declaration of Rights (1776), rest on the unmistakable conviction that civil, political, or legal discrimination on the basis of wealth, ethnic background, or religious affiliation is wrong in the United States because it is wrong everywhere. Thomas Jefferson could not have made this point clearer when he wrote to James Madison in 1787: "A bill of rights is what the people are entitled to against every government on earth, general or particular; and what no just government should refuse, or rest on inference."[13]

Jefferson's claim does not support the idea that the fundamental rights of human beings are subject to cultural or ethnic variation, having one meaning in one society and the opposite in another. A belief in universal human rights, including a universal opportunity for an improved standard of living and for the development of a democratic political system, resides at the core of the basic institutional commitments and loyalties—the basic valuables—of the American Republic.

To hold nations accountable to a universal standard of morality puts appeals to national security in a new light. Governments are not quite so free to define their security as they see fit. Certainly, in the minds of America's Founders, the pursuit of national security must be directed and restrained by the basic moral commitments of constitutional government. National security is not independent of morality, but is defined and confined by morality. Thus, governments are required to prove that they are not using the excuse of national emergency as a pretext for suppressing the universal rights of citizens. James Madison, in a 1789 letter to Jefferson at the height of the hysteria that produced the Alien and Sedition Acts, wrote: "Perhaps it is a universal truth that the loss of liberty at home is to be charged to provisions against danger, real or pretended, from abroad." Precisely because they knew that the excuse of national security is easily abused, Madison and Jefferson were devoted to institutionalizing accountability in government. They believed that political power must always be restrained by morality.

It is apparent that the chasm between the ideas of Thomas Jefferson and James Madison and the ideas of George Kennan is wide. For Kennan, values such as human rights, improved living conditions, and democracy are a matter of cultural or ethnic preference; they are "relative," as he has said more than once. Concern for national security properly takes little cognizance of such values. He contends that if a nation, in the pursuit of national security, must systematically contradict its moral ideals—if it must subvert the human rights of its own or other nations' citizens—then it should do so, where indicated, unflinchingly, for such is the way of the world.

For Jefferson and Madison, by contrast, to consider national security without remaining conscious of the basic rights and privileges of a free people is repugnant. The purpose of a "just government" is to protect those rights and privileges when necessary, by military and other means, and, moreover, to protect them, when possible and feasible, for all peoples everywhere, not just for American citizens. For the Founders, the ultimate and invariant standards for measuring force or any other means required for maintaining a nation's security are universal moral principles. As I have suggested, that is a fundamental assumption on which the American Revolution was based.

Morality, Realism, and the Necessity Defense

At this point, I must admit that Kennan's arguments have hardly been disposed of. He would rejoin that it is just this kind of dreamy sentimentalism, associated with a rather innocent and naive universalism—a view no doubt espoused by the Founders—that he is trying to overcome. It is just this sort of moralism, Kennan might say, that produces the misadventures of a Woodrow Wilson. Such an outlook is as irrelevant to the real world as it is mischievous: it prompts either reckless adventurism in the name of some moral crusade or, equally harmful, inspires faintheartedness and tender conscience—attributes that impede undertaking the necessary, if morally objectionable, action. As "realists," Kennan and his followers deny that the world of international relations is susceptible to high-sounding moral principles.

In his book on the CIA, Woodward provides an arresting example of the passion for realism. From the early days of the Reagan administration, William Casey was attracted to covert operations in combating terrorists such as Mumar Qaddafi. He was particularly eager to funnel arms, money, political support, and technical assistance to Chad's Defense Minister, Hissène Habré, as a way of ridding Chad of Qaddafi's influence. The trouble was that Habré himself was a deeply questionable chap, apparently involved in massacring his fellow citizens. Consequently, both the CIA and the House Intelligence Committee had been insistent about preventing Habré from using lethal aid against his own political opposition. "This human-rights nicety," writes Woodward, "was a big issue in the congressional oversight committees." But, typically, Casey disdained such scruples. "'God damn,' Casey responded, 'did they want a note from Habré's mother: Habré was a brutal, calculating survivor.... Where was the realism?'"[14]

A dose of realism about the world of international affairs is indispensable, and we are indebted to realists for continuing to point out the foibles and misadventures of the "moralist" tradition. To some extent, intelligence gathering, espionage, covert activities, and the use of armed force in order to "insure domestic tranquility" and "provide for the common defense"—as the Constitution guarantees—must go on. Awareness of that fact helps to prevent leaders from imprudent adventurism, on the one hand, and self-defeating timidity, on the other.

However, to make this concession is not necessarily to accept Kennan's penchant for severing all ties between national security and morality. The tradition of moral reflection out of which Jefferson and Madison fashioned their ideas allowed considerable room for moral excuse-making—a procedure that specifically applies to the sorts of vexing cases that arise in the course of competition and discord among nations.

That tradition fully recognized that circumstances of deep moral conflict occasionally exist in which, for example, the right to life of one individual or collectivity excludes the equivalent right to life of another individual or collectivity. The standard illustration is of two people after a shipwreck contending for a plank of wood that can support only one of them, or of two mothers with enough food to sustain only one of their infants. The same conditions apply collectively to a struggle for survival between two groups, as, for example, between the Israelis and the Palestinians over mutually exclusive territorial claims.[15]

Such circumstances are typically described as *cases of necessity*. These are cases in which at least some ordinary moral rules do not apply because, in the name of survival, it is "necessary" to override conventional prohibitions.

It is important to emphasize that such circumstances are morally circumscribed. People who invoke the "necessity defense" shoulder a heavy burden of proof. They must provide evidence that they are, in fact, confronted with a dilemma of this sort, and that they have conscientiously endeavored to operate within the limits imposed by the defense.

The burden of proof is heavy because the tradition readily recognizes how liable to abuse the necessity defense is. As Madison's comment, cited earlier, insinuates, governments seem universally tempted to invoke this excuse at the drop of a hat, to use it as a pretext for committing all sorts of unconscionable acts. Because the defense is intended to serve, not to oppose, moral objectives, that temptation is particularly ominous. To misapply the excuse—deliberately or negligently—is a highly reprehensible moral violation.

Up to a point, Kennan's approach to the subject of morality and national security is simply an application of the necessity defense. For Kennan and his followers, virtually all international politics pits right against right, life against life. Therefore, crucial foreign policy decisions and actions must be conceived of as matters of necessity. In this context, according to Kennan, standard moral rules are set aside. Morally speaking, decisions about national security are always exceptional.

But there is, as we say, more to the defense than that. Because it permits exceptions to ordinary moral rules, the necessity defense compensates by imposing exacting requirements of accountability, all in the name, finally, of protecting morality. Kennan ignores this second part. That is why his position is so different from Madison's. That is why Kennan lacks Madison's passion to curtail the use of the necessity defense, lest in the guise of an appeal to security a government undermine the fundamental rights and freedoms—the moral commitments—of just government.

Kennan can hardly be held responsible for America's rather dismal record of cultivating appropriate restrictions and restraints on the use of the necessity defense during national crises. Nor is he entirely to blame for an underdeveloped sense of skepticism toward appeals to national security in this country's history. At the same time, his ideas do not provide the direction and impetus needed to correct this record.

Justice William J. Brennan, Jr., in discussing the experience of the United States with the suspension of civil liberties in times of security crises, demonstrates just how unflattering the record is. He contends that although the nation has accomplished much in the protection of human rights for its citizens, "[t]here is considerably less to be proud about, and a good deal to be embarrassed about, when one reflects on the shabby treatment civil liberties have received in the U.S. during times of war and perceived threats to its national security."[16]

After reviewing the disturbing circumstances surrounding the Alien and Sedition Acts of 1798, Lincoln's dubious suspension of the writ of habeas corpus during the Civil War, and the arbitrary internment of over 100,000 Japanese resident aliens and Japanese-Americans during

World War II, Brennan derives three sobering lessons. The record, he says,

> teaches [first] that abstract principles announcing the applicability of civil liberties during times of war and crisis are ineffectual when a war or other crisis comes along unless the principles are fleshed out by a detailed jurisprudence explaining how those civil liberties will be sustained against particularized national security concerns. It teaches [second] that—procedures for swiftly enforcing that jurisprudence during times of calamity must also be designed and implemented, lest the jurisprudence perpetually find itself providing guidance only in retrospect. Finally, it teaches that the perceived threats to national security that have motivated the sacrifice of civil liberties during times of crisis are often overblown and factually unfounded.[17]

Kennan's line of thinking runs in a very different direction from Brennan's. By abstracting the notion of national security from the fabric of moral commitments and ideals for which the United States stands and then elevating that abstraction to the preeminent principle for guiding foreign policy, Kennan undercuts the basis for rigorous restraints on appeals to national security that Brennan calls for.

International Legal Restraints

It is relevant to note that Justice Brennan's recommendations have already begun to be realized in the international community by means of some of the articles contained in human rights and humanitarian law. Several of the major international and regional documents—such as the International Covenant on Civil and Political Rights, the European and Inter-American Conventions on Human Rights, and the four Geneva Conventions governing conditions of armed conflict—make provisions, within strict limits, for suspending certain human rights under conditions of public emergency.[18]

For example, Article 4 of the International Covenant on Civil and Political Rights states:

> 1. In time of public emergency which threatens the life of the nation and the existence of which is officially proclaimed, the States Parties to the present Covenant may take measures derogating from [suspending] their obligations to the extent strictly required by the exigencies of the situation, provided that such measures are not inconsistent with their other obligations under international law and do not involve discrimination solely on the ground of race, colour, sex, language, religion or social origin.

> 2. No derogation from articles 6 [against arbitrary deprivation of life], 7 [against torture or cruel, inhuman or degrading treatment or punishment], 8 (paragraphs 1 and 2) [against slavery and servitude], 11 [against imprisonment for inability to fulfill contractual obligation], 15 [against retroactive laws], 16 [for legal recognition "everywhere"], and 18 [for freedom of thought, conscience and religion, and the liberty to "manifest" these beliefs in action, subject to certain specified limitations] may be made under this provision.

> 3. Any State Party to the present Covenant availing itself of the right of derogation shall immediately inform the other States Parties to the present Covenant, through the intermediary of the Secretary-General of the United Nations, of the provisions from which it has derogated and of the reasons by which it was actuated. A further communication shall be made, through the same intermediary, on the date on which it terminates the derogation.[19]

Accordingly, the international documents give legal form to the skepticism and suspicion expressed by James Madison and Justice Brennan toward the use of appeals to "states of exception." By endeavoring to hem in such appeals through various procedures and standards, the instruments are true to the moral tradition within which the necessity defense is properly understood. They begin to encourage, in the spirit of Justice Brennan's remarks, the "disciplining" of appeals to national security.

A Universal Morality?

At this point, Kennan and his followers are likely to register one final objection, which is surely profound: How is it possible to prove the universal validity of the American view of morality? Is it clear that American interpretations of these valuables are of interest or use to people in other traditions? Who appointed the United States moral tutor of the universe?

Two primary considerations prepare the way for answering this question. First, it was not particularly prescient of Kennan to have pictured such a great divide between the United States and Asia, as he did in his memorandum in 1947. Since then, Japan has become a relatively mature and successful democracy, and as such, something of a model for other Asian countries. South Korea, Taiwan, and the Philippines are struggling democracies, to be sure, but they are countries for which constitutional protections, human rights, and improved and equitable living conditions have become matters of urgent public debate.

These circumstances are not limited to Asia. Although it is more difficult to find success stories in black Africa, one of the most interesting features of the postcolonial African nations is the degree to which they have internalized the cultural and political struggles that were bred to a large extent during the colonial era. Invoking universal human rights and the claims of democratic self-determination in the effort to shed their colonial masters, many African countries became constitutional democracies, at least in form. They thereby began a painful cultural struggle to harmonize and coordinate the norms of human rights and democracy with other traditions and customs indigenous to their cultures.

The struggle continues today and the final consequences remain unknown. However, to claim that human rights, improved living conditions, and democratization have no bearing on the lives of the inhabitants of these countries is surely mistaken. The same pattern has occurred in other areas of the world. These facts alone suggest grounds for skepticism of Kennan's assertion that the moral concerns of the United States are totally irrelevant to the concerns of other peoples and other cultures.

Second, it is useful to test Kennan's version of moral relativism. Is it possible to live content with the idea that basic human rights are good for Americans and similar people, but irrelevant to others? The following case, taken from Bob Woodward's book, sharply poses this question in relation to considerations of national security.

Woodward explains that because of William Casey's passion for waging counterterrorism, he was eager to develop Lebanese units and, gradually, to expand the program to other countries. The main purpose of these units was to engage in "preemptive attacks" against terrorist leaders. One such leader was the notorious Sheikh Fadlallah, leader of *Hezbollah*, the Party of God. Through Casey's contacts with the Saudis, such a unit was created. "On March 8, 1985," writes Woodward,

> a car packed with explosives was driven into a Beirut suburb about fifty yards from Fadlallah's high-rise residence. The car exploded, killing eighty people and wounding two hundred, leaving devastation, fires and collapsed buildings. Anyone who had happened to be in the immediate neighborhood was killed, hurt, or terrorized, but Fadlallah escaped without injury.[20]

Assuming that observers would regard the operation as a failure, the question is, Why is it considered so? There are three possible responses. It might be judged unsatisfactory simply because Fadlallah escaped; presumably the operation would have been a "success" if Fadlallah had died along with the others. Second, the operation might be considered a failure because it was indiscriminate; even if Fadlallah had been killed, the operation would still have been misguided because innocent people lost their lives or were injured.

Third, the operation might be regarded as unsatisfactory simply because it was undertaken at all. This third response was apparently that of Casey's subordinates. For example, John McMahon held such missions to be inherently uncontrollable: they were nothing more than assassination attempts, actions ruled out by presidential executive order.[21]

Most observers would probably select the second or third responses: the attack was unsatisfactory because it was indiscriminate, or because it was the kind of act that is itself hard to distinguish from terrorism. When selecting those responses, does the nationality of the victims—whether Lebanese, Nigerian, or Filipino—matter? Or does it matter that the perpetrators were American, British, Saudi, or Lebanese (all of whom, incidentally, were accomplices in the action)?

When lethal force is used indiscriminately, such an action appears to be wrong in itself, or universally wrong— wrong, that is, for anyone anywhere to do to anyone anywhere. From this point of view, every human being is assumed, at the very least, to have a human right against being "arbitrarily deprived of . . . life," as is stated in Article 4 of the Inter-American Convention.[22]

Containing and preventing the arbitrary use of force is a fundamental and absolute moral requirement. Because it is absolute, it may not be overridden by appeals to anything, including appeals to national security. Actions that willfully or negligently violate the prohibition against arbitrary force, as did, apparently, the assault on Fadlallah's apartment building, are categorically indefensible.

This is only one example of a universal moral restriction that would be imposed on all acts, even acts undertaken in the name of national security. Granted, it is a long jump from this sort of minimal moral constraint to a developed set of human rights, such as are contained in the international documents, or to an elaborate system of procedures and standards to prevent abuse of national security appeals, such as Justice Brennan calls for.

Nevertheless, the example serves to counter Kennan's penchant for divorcing affairs of state from moral considerations. If the above analysis is correct, there are potent reasons against driving too large a wedge between morality and national security. There are equally strong reasons not to ignore those ideals and moral commitments that are an inextricable part of the national valuables the nation is bound to secure.

Notes

1. George F. Kennan, *Sketches From a Life* (New York: Pantheon Books, 1990).

2. "Review of Current Trends, U.S. Foreign Policy," PPS/23, Top Secret. Included in *Foreign Relations of the United States, 1948* (Washington, D.C.: Government Printing Office, 1976), vol. I, part 2, pp. 509–29; cited in Raymond Bonner, *Waltzing with a Dictator: The Marcoses and the Making of American Policy* (New York: Times Books, 1987), p. 33.

3. George F. Kennan, "Morality and Foreign Policy," *Foreign Affairs* 64, no. 2 (Winter 1985/86): 205–18. (Reprinted as an appendix to this volume.)

4. George F. Kennan, *Realities of American Foreign Policy* (New York and Oxford: Oxford University Press, 1954), p. 47.

5. See Kennan, "Morality and Foreign Policy," p. 206.

6. Kennan, *Realities of American Foreign Policy*, p. 49.

7. In distinguishing interests and morality so sharply, Kennan stands squarely in the tradition of Thomas Hobbes. For Hobbes, religion or morality was the source of antagonism and conflict. Recognition of what human beings hold in common— their mutual need for self-preservation—is the only secure foundation for peace and stability.

8. Bob Woodward, *Veil: The Secret Wars of the CIA, 1981–87* (New York: Simon & Schuster, 1987), p. 124.

9. Claire Sterling, *The Terror Network: The Secret War of International Terrorism* (New York: Holt, Rhinehart, 1981).

10. Woodward, *Veil*, p. 125.

11. Richard H. Ullman, "Redefining Security," *International Security* 8, no. 1 (Summer 1983): 133.

12. Harold Lasswell and Abraham Kaplan, *Power and Society: A Framework for Political Inquiry* (New Haven: Yale University Press, 1950), p. 61.

13. Thomas Jefferson to James Madison, December 20, 1787, in Arienne Koch and William Peden, eds., *Life and Selected Writings of Thomas Jefferson* (New York: Random House, 1944).

14. Woodward, *Veil*, p. 157.

15. I have analyzed the history and current understanding of the necessity defense in the international community at greater length in a forthcoming book, "Rights and Emergencies: Protecting Human Rights in the Midst of Conflict."

16. William J. Brennan, Jr., "The Quest to Develop a Jurisprudence of Civil Liberties in Times of Security Crises," *Israel Yearbook of Human Rights*, vol. 18, 1988 (Dordrecht: Martinus Nijhoff Publishers, 1988), pp. 11–21.

17. Ibid., pp. 11–12.

18. In addition to Article 4 of the International Covenant on Civil and Political Rights, see the European Convention on Human Rights, Article 15, and the American Convention on Human Rights, Article 27, for the "derogation clauses," or articles relating to public emergency. Analogous examples of limits placed on appeals to "military necessity" are scattered throughout the Geneva Conventions of 1949, for example, Convention I, Article 50. For the text of these conventions see *Human Rights Documents* (Committee on Foreign Affairs, U.S. House of Representatives, U.S. Government Printing Office, 1983), pp. 177, 195, and 339.

19. Ibid., p. 80.

20. Woodward, *Veil*, p. 397.

21. Ibid., p. 398.

22. *Human Rights Documents*, p. 170.

Universal Morality

I would like to respond to David Little's paper by way of parables and anecdotes; I come from a culture where they are a tool of communication. I offer my anecdotes to make two principal points: first, the issue of societal values and the scope of their relevance, and second, the role of leadership in widening the relevance of societal values.

My first anecdote concerns a study I conducted some years ago. My field of study was law and, in the Yale Law School tradition, I tried to see the interconnection between law, science, and policy to discover some of the fundamental objectives or values that law was supposed to promote in a society. After I had documented my arguments about traditional law by using cases to illustrate the broadly defined values that I remembered from my childhood and early life in Dinka society, I thought it would be interesting to collect folktales as a means of substantiating the value systems that law is supposed to reflect and promote. I was fascinated to find that the folktales I read had similarities with tales I had heard as a child. Looking at them again as a student of society, I became so intrigued by what they told me that my first accomplishment on a postdoctoral fellowship at Yale Law School was to write a book of folktales.

One fascinating theme in those tales was the interaction between the worlds of humans and animals. One after another demonstrated that there was a certain point at which violations of basic human and social values resulted in the transformation of human habits into those of animals—in most cases, a lion's. Usually, that transformation took place through interaction with lions, who were capable of portraying humans, or appearing to be human beings, and, at a critical phase, influencing humans to the point where humans were transformed into lions. The humans turned-lions were then either beaten and punished in various ways such that they became humans again or they were killed without remorse because they were considered animals.

The lions symbolized foreigners; their habits as described in the folktales reflected some of the same patterns we see today among the neighbors of the Dinka. The present-day application is that the moral context of the Dinka people, centered on their own immediate group, broadens until it reaches a point where it is forced to interact with the outside world, represented by the animals.

The other anecdote I would like to relate regards an experience I had in England in 1963, when I witnessed Lyndon Johnson, then vice president, being interviewed on the BBC. In his interview he said that Americans do not fully realize how blessed they are, and that, although the world criticizes Americans, the criticism has nothing to do with anything Americans do wrong; its source is the envy, jealousy, and hatred other people feel toward the blessings of Americans. When I heard this, I did not question the facts. I was, however, surprised to hear a world leader say, through a medium that was heard everywhere, that Americans were the ideal and that the rest of the world was wrong in its perception of America. Three days later, then-Vice President Johnson became president, following the assassination of President Kennedy. To my pleasant surprise, the BBC apologized for having aired that interview.

I suppose it would be making a big jump, but I think it is fair to say that every society has basic values around which it structures its social relationships and the whole purpose of its life. Underlying most of these value systems are fundamental principles of human dignity, expressed in many ways and perhaps realized in varying degrees, but essentially universal. I make this observation based on the comparative work that I have done on African traditional societies.

In translating some of the words used to describe the Dinka value system, I have often found myself using the concept of the *gentleman*. In the Dinka system, *gentleman* is a word that connotes very precise, detailed ideas relating to personal mannerisms, relationships with other human beings, and deferential as well as welfare values. My editors would often ask, "Are you sure you mean *gentleman*?" and I would wonder why they asked. Their reaction was based on the assumption that the word *gentleman* is peculiar to the English language and associated with certain behavior patterns that are culturally relative. The fact that the Dinka word *gentleman* has more positive, substantive content than the class notion of being a gentleman does in English did not occur to the editors. In other words, they could not imagine that a traditional African society might think in terms of a gentleman.

Three questions come to mind at this point. First, what aspect of this complex value system does a society choose as its main overriding value? For instance, we know that in traditional African society, values associated with the lineage system, the patrilineal line, kinship ties, and the notion of continuity through children—a form of immortality—become so central that life is seen in those terms. Thus, in the case of murder, cattle are used for payment to compensate for the dead, as a means to acquire a wife and beget children, all in the name of the dead person. In contrast, in the Western world, property values are so highly prized that much of what happens is a consequence of that premise. So, there is a relative choice of priorities.

The second question is, Who within a particular social context benefits from those values? Again we find disparities in the distribution or sharing of those values where descent (family ties, that is), age, or sex are factors.

The third question concerns the scope of the application of those values, and that is where my story about Dinka folktales comes into the picture. How do those moral postulates relate to the framework of foreign policy? I believe that it may be true to say that foreign policy is more of an attempt to promote domestic concerns in foreign circles than to promote true foreign relations, which means, therefore, that the main objectives within the domestic framework determine the priorities in the foreign context.

So the values that preoccupy a society, that the society strives to live up to, are promoted in the external context such that the human values identified in the external context become an extension of the internal. Let me illustrate with a specific case of my country. In the Sudan, the former President Jaafar Mohamed Nimeiri, for reasons of pragmatism and self-interest, negotiated an agreement that brought peace after seventeen years of war with the Southern Sudan Liberation Movement. Africa hailed the agreement as a great accomplishment for the continent, an example of what many countries needed to emulate. Sudan used that achievement as a basis for winning friendships around the world. For example, I was appointed ambassador to Scandinavia to display that positive accomplishment as a basis for winning the friendships of those countries that had been concerned about the war in the southern Sudan.

I pursued the same role as ambassador to Washington, and even as minister of state. The accomplishment definitively conveyed the idea that Sudan was now well placed to play a constructive role in the regional objectives of peace—to be a mediator, to take or support initiatives—and it was in that context that Sudan was the only Arab country that supported the Camp David Accords.

My other example points to President Carter's placing human rights on the U.S. foreign policy agenda. I witnessed firsthand the enormous impact that action had on the attitudes of African governments, including my own country's. I saw Nimeiri endorse the human rights agenda with enthusiasm because he knew it would endear him to the leaders in Washington. When he realized that U.S. foreign policy objectives had shifted with the change of administration in Washington and that ideological priorities were now determining friendships, he reversed his endorsement: the domestic scene in terms of human rights was altered, and the threat from Libya and Marxist Ethiopia became his basis for winning Washington's friendship.

Therefore, it seems to me that when we speak of the relevance of morals to foreign policy, we have to recognize the widening circles that extend beyond the world of Dinka folktales. Even in Sudan, I have witnessed in my lifetime the transformation of tribes, from thinking of the world as within a limited framework, to endorsing neighbors as part of the same framework and, ultimately, the nation as a whole. Although there is still much to be desired, the framework of the nation, seen as endorsing all human beings as human beings, has become a reality—a reality to be improved on, but a reality, nonetheless.

The challenge in today's world is that although the circles broaden to include international organizations and we witness all kinds of resolutions as evidence, those resolutions are not implemented. However, because the resolutions define the framework of human dignity in broader terms, at least we are moving in the right direction.

What is needed, then, is leadership. Leadership within the Sudanese framework first broadened vision from the tribal to the broader intertribal and, then, national context. Leadership brought about major transformations in the case of Sudan, and it is the failure of leadership that has set us back.

In the case of the United States, there is an inevitable leadership role that is related to the statement made by the late President Lyndon Johnson and some of the things that

David Little has said. Such are the challenges facing leaders all over the world and, in particular, the leaders of the superpowers.

THEODORE WEBER

What Kennan Really Said

I agree with David Little that one cannot really separate politics and morality. When I hear arguments to the effect that they must be separated, I usually find that there is a superficial understanding of politics, on one side, and of morality, on the other, and that persons who are making that claim do not pay enough attention to the presuppositions of their own thinking or to the character of their rhetoric, which often is moral rhetoric.

Having said that, I think Little has overstated the case for George Kennan as a consistent political amoralist. I am well aware of Kennan's arguments about keeping morality separate from politics, but one has to look at the context to understand what he means.

First, we should recognize that he is talking mainly about the ends, not the means, of foreign policy. I cannot imagine that Kennan would disagree with Little's statement about the terrorist attack sponsored indirectly by the United States in Beirut; I think he would have condemned that. If you have some citation that shows I am mistaken, I would like to see it. I think that Kennan is committed to universals of the type you suggest, with regard to questions of means. In support of that argument, I point to his book *Nuclear Delusion*, in which he writes about nuclear weapons and states his position: he has been against them from the beginning.[1] His position is based not only on strategic considerations but also on moral ones.

Kennan expresses a great deal of moral outrage over the casual way in which certain states with strategic responsibilities talk about taking out other states' cities, and he says, in effect, "We simply cannot talk in terms like that. These people are *people*, are children of God, created in the image of God the same as we are." He uses theological language to support his moral argument. And there are other statements in the nuclear discussion showing that he is very much concerned about the means, not simply the ends, of foreign policy.

However, when he talks about the purposes of foreign policy, it is true that he does make the kind of separation Little refers to. Kennan is noted for that distinction. He has, as Little has pointed out, argued that we should proceed in terms of power relationships and national interests, not in terms of democratization and human rights, as ends of foreign policy. Little has given some of the reasons that Kennan offers. One is that we run the risk of messianism when we set out to convert the world to our system or to require the rest of the world to accept our value system, and that, of course, is a moral concern.

Kennan would also argue, as Reinhold Niebuhr often argued, that we simply do not know enough about other cultures to be able to identify the kind of system they need. We have to be more humble in that regard, and humility is a moral virtue. When we go on moral crusades to convert or democratize other people, it may really be the case that we are pursuing our own interests and not theirs. That is a warning that Kennan, Niebuhr, Morgenthau, and others would give.

The main point, however, is that when we think of the argument Kennan makes—although I am thinking of Kennan in terms of the arguments he made in the late 1940s and early 1950s and in his book *American Diplomacy*—he is not simply saying "pursue national interests," although he does say that; he is arguing in terms of a particular geopolitical model of the world, the way in which the world is set up, the relationships among states that are a projection of geography and power and are historically established.[2] The geopolitical model has a history, and as such, it creates a set of expectations on the basis of which states react to each other.

In *American Diplomacy*, much of Kennan's chastising of American moralism had to do with the fact that American diplomats, in his view, were not paying attention to the geopolitical model with its associated expectations. Instead, they were setting forth ideal models, moral principle models. Other states would hear such talk and respond, "Oh, come on, they can't really mean that. Just as England and France have carved out their spheres of influence, so will the United States; this talk of morality is just window-dressing. So we had better find out what their power objectives are, and respond to those."

But some American statesmen really believed that they were acting on the basis of moral principle, and they wanted to sweep away all other considerations as they attempted to establish new arrangements that would correspond to their moral visions.

Kennan criticized that kind of diplomacy because it violated the expectations that were part of the system, and in doing so, it produced bad politics that were also, in his view, immoral; that is to say, to proceed without an understanding of the geopolitical model is morally irresponsible. By making an argument for the separation of morality and politics, he was making an argument for political responsibility, which is a moral category. This understanding must be borne in mind when portrayals of George Kennan create the impression that he is making an absolute separation between morality and politics and insisting that one has nothing to do with the other.

He does make that separation, but it has a contextual meaning; he is talking about political responsibility developed out of moral sensitivity, and, of course, Kennan is morally a very sensitive person. I say this not to enter into his defense, but rather to make the point that politics and morality are best understood in the context of their relationship.

What matters more than relating universals to political reality is recognizing the relationship between values and principles and state responsibility for the attempt to civilize or politicize military relationships. What I mean by "state responsibility" is that persons who hold office ought to have a sense of responsibility for fulfilling the expectations of that office. Most of the people whom I have known personally or known about feel that they hold office with a sense of moral responsibility. Jimmy Carter and Ronald Reagan feel that way, even though there are profound differences between them; in principle, they agree that the president of the United States has the moral responsibility to look after the interests of the nation.

Now, that is part of political morality, but it is not the whole of it, because if one raises the question of responsibility, one must also ask: Are there responsibilities, in addition to the responsibilities of office, for territory and people? Are there responsibilities that are incumbent upon our actions and that we must heed in the course of discharging the duties of this office? To this question one could answer yes; there are other responsibilities, and at a minimum, they are responsibilities to those other persons or states who are affected in any way by our exercise of power. This is a necessary, politically and morally meaningful qualification on national interests that arises from the notion of responsibility.

To decide where to draw the line for responsibility is fundamentally a religious decision. What I mean is this: if we say we are responsible only to our own people, we are deciding that our people have more value than other people in the world. This decision is not just a matter of saying politics works this way; it is a specific religious decision made on the basis of a faith that is then put into political practice.

But if we say, as Kennan has said, that we do have responsibility to other people and, therefore, we cannot incinerate them, that is a religious decision of a different order that necessarily informs the political practice. The politicization of the military is also of central importance because the picture of the world that we may have—and the picture that Kennan often had—is a picture of nations that are matching each other with weapons in the name of security. That is a real aspect of the world, but it is not the only one, as Kennan knows. The politicization of relationships therefore means building connective tissues above and beyond the military relationship so that states do not have to rely only on military relationships when dealing with each other; it means building diplomatic relationships to contain and control military relationships. I do not believe it means going as far as world government. Some people would disagree with me, but I think that, even if world government were a good idea, it is not a likely possibility.

Politicization means bringing interstate relationships under political control so that everything is not reduced to military considerations. It is an expression of political responsibility in the real world where national interest is involved, politics are taken seriously, and the context is provided for raising questions of values, human rights, and democracy, such that these values are raised not as universals but within the context of political operations.

Notes

1. George F. Kennan, *The Nuclear Delusion* (New York: Pantheon Books, 1983).

2. George F. Kennan, *American Diplomacy* (Chicago: University of Chicago Press, 1984).

RICHARD JOSEPH

Power and Ethics in the Third World

My remarks concern the struggle between the superpowers during the cold war and the consequences this struggle has had for Africa, in particular, but also for other parts of the world. This morning I was in a meeting that dealt with the conflicts in the Horn of Africa; we focused on Sudan and Ethiopia. We looked at the possibilities of ending the destructive conflicts there and also at the whole issue of the use of food as an instrument of war, the deliberate creation of hunger and famine. I think this discussion relates very much to the issue of superpower conflicts.

Let me refer briefly to a *New York Times* article by Thomas Friedman in which he talks about the superpowers' taking their cold war home with them, away from various regions of the world. He says that as the Soviet Union has begun to reduce involvement in certain regional conflicts, the United States has done the same, because its interests in various countries are often the result of Moscow's backing of the other side.

This tendency to define U.S. interests in terms of Moscow's, which we have done throughout the postwar era, coincided with the emergence of many African nations and their struggles for independence. This tendency has been highly destructive of those nations; they are affected by a policy that says if the Russians are *for* a particular government, then we must be for those people fighting *against* the government, and vice versa.

During my early years of studies in Africa, I remember having to deal with issues of selective assassination, the imprisonment of political opponents, censorship, and all kinds of moral abuses. These abuses took place in countries that were strong allies of the United States; they voted with us in the United Nations. Therefore, those issues of abuse were treated as irrelevant.

The question I raise is whether the end of the cold war, which many of us feel is approaching, means that we can now move toward an ethically based foreign policy, especially with regard to Africa. I want to describe what I mean by "ethically based" in a very down-to-earth way. With us here today is Jack Shepherd, a former journalist and current professor at Dartmouth College, who wrote about the famine that took place in Ethiopia in 1984 and participated in the discussion this morning. I suspect you are all familiar with pictures of the starving people in Ethiopia, but Shepherd played a very important role in sounding the alarm about the extent to which the United States was unwilling to provide food aid because the government at the time—the Mengistu regime—happened to be allied with the Soviet Union. Shepherd quotes a senior aid official: "It is naive to assume that food aid has as its major purpose the alleviation of hunger and poverty. To give food to countries just because people are starving is a pretty weak reason." I think most people would recognize this position as realist and, in a very fundamental way, immoral.

At a meeting here at the Carter Center in April 1988 there was a delegation of Russian specialists, a number of them from the Moscow-based Institute of African Studies. They recognized that they supported their dictators in Africa, we supported ours, and that the United States and the Soviet Union could now avoid situations such as when the

United States—which had long supported Ethiopia—
switched its support to Somalia because Ethiopia turned
Communist.

What would it mean for the superpowers to move away
from that kind of behavior? It would mean, for example, that
instead of using aid competitively, because of our rival national interests, we could now use aid directly to improve the
lives of people.

An expert from the Soviet Foreign Ministry suggested
that perhaps the United States and the Soviet Union could
work cooperatively to help develop Namibia (after its an-
ticipated independence) instead of making Namibia the object of competitive aid, security, and other kinds of actions,
as has been the case with many countries in Africa.

A nonethical approach to foreign policy has been very
closely tied to the cold war. The end of the cold war—especially with regard to areas such as Africa, which is suffering
tremendously—opens the possibility for those of us who
want to raise moral issues not to be accused of moral rhetoric
and crusades, in the words of Professor Weber. Such accusa-
tions only attach a lot of negatives to the question of morality;
instead, I hope that we can deal with morality in its true
sense—the pursuit of the greater good of the people.

DAYLE E. POWELL

Equal Necessity

Perhaps what has been wrong with U.S. foreign policy over the past 200 years is that, for the most part, it has been made by men. Perhaps if there were more women making foreign policy we would not be having this debate now. By saying that, my point of departure is not a man's, but a woman's. I commend to you a wonderful book by Sissela Bok, called *A Strategy for Peace.*[1] I hope you will read this book, along with those by George Kennan.

Bok tells the story of an incident that happened during the Peloponnesian War, when an ambassador from Athens went to the island of Milos to deliver an ultimatum: either surrender, or be slaughtered and enslaved. In response to that ultimatum, the people of the island pleaded for mercy and justice. The famous debate that ensued in those few minutes on the island of Milos resulted in the following exchange: "Just solutions are sought only when both sides are under equal necessity; otherwise, the powerful do what they have the power to do while the weak accept what they have to accept."[2] This proposition is often cited rather cynically, for it expresses the idea that in the politics of power and self-interest, nations speak of justice only when they cannot prevail by force, and that the talk of justice is simply that, nothing but talk.

It seems to me that in this age the prospect of a nuclear Sarajevo places all of us under equal necessity; therefore, I think that the manner in which we must deal with issues like national security and ethics is changed. It is important for us to realize that there has been a major shift in the way the nations make war since 1945. Since that time, with the exception of the Persian Gulf war, there have not been any major, all-out international conflicts. Instead, nations have fought civil wars.

Today's civil war—twenty-three of which are being fought this week, if we define a war as a conflict in which more than 1,000 lives are lost per year—is typically started by rebels who want to change the racial balance of power in the country, or who want to secede from the union in which they find themselves. Seventeen million people have died in such wars since 1945; most recently, three-fourths of those deaths have occurred on Asian and African soil. Perhaps the reason the American population is not familiar with these conflicts is because it is convenient for us to wear blinders with respect to these issues. We do not have to confront them; we are not directly affected by them.

I submit the proposition that humanity can no longer accept the existence of war as inevitable or preordained. I believe there have been many positive examples of innovative approaches being taken to deal with important conflicts of our time. I would list, for instance, the Solidarity movement in Poland, where the fight for freedom and human rights has been waged without spears or guns; Gandhi in India; Martin Luther King in Atlanta and Birmingham; and Corazon Aquino in the Philippines. In all of these instances, nonviolent resistance was used to achieve social change without hatred, without battles, and without the risk of escalation into nuclear conflict.

What are called for now are innovative approaches to the way we resolve our conflicts—approaches that do not accept war as an option; that teach us to separate more effectively the person with whom we are in dispute from the problem, and to separate that person's position from his underlying needs and interests; and that, in our approach to national security issues, help us focus on finding ways to meet the needs of both sides through a negotiated approach. Only with this new and much-needed approach to the way we resolve our conflicts can we expect another century on this earth; only this way can we avoid being blighted by some horrible nuclear incident.

If an international standard for morality is applicable, I suggest that we look not to George Kennan but to Immanuel Kant's *Perpetual Peace*, written in 1795, wherein he suggested this premise: people—singly and collectively—should act as if their actions constitute international law, so that their daily interactions are judged by the same standard that is applied on an international level.[3] If states were to conduct their behavior in their dealings with other nations in this way— that is, if they were to apply the same standard internationally and nationally—I believe we would have an appropriate balance between morality and national security.

Notes

1. Sissela Bok, *A Strategy for Peace* (New York: Pantheon Books, 1989).

2. Ibid., p. 21.

3. Immanuel Kant, "Perpetual Peace: A Philosophical Sketch," in Hans Reiss, ed., *Kant's Political Writings* (Cambridge: Cambridge University Press, 1970).

A Discussion of Morality and Foreign Policy

David Little: I appreciate these very illuminating comments. Let me respond briefly to Ted Weber, as he was the only one among the panelists who took issue with what I said about Kennan. I believe Kennan is a complex person and I should acknowledge that he makes many different points on the subject of national security and morality. However, I do not believe he is quite as clear on these issues as you have portrayed him to be, Ted. I do not think he consistently makes the distinctions between means and ends that you suggest. I have searched his writings for such distinctions, and I have never found a careful or developed application of them.

I believe that George Kennan uses a blunderbuss, rather than a scalpel, when talking about moral matters, and we are thereby worse off. An argument along the lines of Ted Weber's that brings some system and consistency to Kennan's line of thinking might push things ahead, but I do not think that Kennan himself has provided that.

With regard to Kennan's *Nuclear Delusion*, the argument there is, I think, consistent with my outline of his approach: In the face of the worldwide threat of nuclear destruction, the survival of all nations is in jeopardy. Therefore, necessity itself requires that nations maximize every effort to minimize that threat. National security itself demands it.

The skein that runs through the comments of all the participants is, to me, very exciting: we live in a new international environment, and we need to think in appropriately new ways. "New occasions teach new duties," in the words of a familiar hymn. Whatever efficacy cold war thinking may have had in helping to protect national interests, and in encouraging a view of the world as divided up into good peoples and bad peoples, the terms of international relations are clearly changing as conditions change. One example of this new outlook is that the old thinking has been replaced by discussions that have been influenced by a consideration of human rights.

The information revolution, which encourages comparative judgments among nations, also highlights the interdependence and interconnection of nations. Concerns over environmental issues and human rights, for example, have substantially modified the exclusive preoccupation with national sovereignty and national survival apparent during the nineteenth century and throughout most of this century in the form of the cold war.

We live in a changing environment that imposes a demand for serious moral reflection. From this afternoon's discussion, I have realized that people are already thinking about and shaping the new duties that are called for.

Samuel W. Lewis: I am not a philosopher, as some people on the panel know very well. We had a very useful and interesting exchange, marred only by the fact that there was a bit too much agreement. I would like to encourage less agreement in this half of the discussion.

Although it is very difficult, I would like to put aside for a moment the question of whether human rights is a good ingredient for U.S. policy. I believe that battle has been won with very significant contributions from President Carter, who fought some fairly tough fights on this issue ten years ago with his own bureaucracies. Those of us who were unenlightened will recall with what fervor they put forth a case that seemed less compelling then than it does now. I think the Reagan administration has picked up on the same theme in many areas—certainly with respect to the Soviets—and it has been one area of continuity between the Carter and Reagan administrations, where there were few others.

That does not mean that all the issues are resolved or that the difficult choices have been made with respect to various countries. I am sure many Kennanites are still lurking in the bowels of the State Department, but there are fewer of them. They have also, by this time, recognized that perhaps George Kennan is occasionally wrong.

However, the relationship between morality and foreign policy is a much broader question than has yet been addressed in terms of its practical implications. In his remarks about the Horn of Africa, Richard Joseph introduced the practical issues of the question. I would like to pose to the panelists some provocative questions to get their remarks on a few situations around the world that the president, the next president, or his policymakers will probably, or should, have to confront not only in terms of practical and pragmatic national interests, but—if what David has said and everyone agrees is correct—on moral grounds as well. How is the convenient, consensus thinking we have heard thus far applied to the following cases?

Let us take the civil war in Lebanon. I do not imagine that anyone thinks it is terribly ethical for either side in Lebanon to be shelling civilian populations. You can accept the argument that the Christians brought it all on themselves, that they should have shared power years ago with the Muslims, and you can still think that General Aoun was a bit unwise to take on Syria without accepting the proposition that the Syrians have a right—a moral right—in the name of peace and security in Lebanon and of their national interest, to do what they are doing. What moral issue does the situation in Lebanon today pose for an American leader after he has decided that it does not directly threaten U.S. national interests and recalls the sad history of our efforts in 1984 to intervene in a Lebanese situation that we ill understood?

Or, how about this one: In the late 1970s, the Kurds—a group with a proud national tradition—were carrying out a rebellion, as they have done over the years, to secure self-determination and independence. Unfortunately, part of their people were in Turkey, part were in Iraq, and part were in Iran. They had great difficulty convincing any of those three countries to give up a chunk of their land despite the Kurds' historically well-grounded claim of self-determination.

There was a period during the Shah's regime in which, because Iran and Iraq were at sword points with each other and Iran was then a close ally of the United States, we were clandestinely assisting, with the help of Iran, the Kurdish effort to achieve independence from Iraq. The Israelis were also assisting the Kurds, both because we were assisting them and because the Kurdish rebellion served Israel's interests.

At a certain point, Iran and Iraq temporarily resolved their border dispute. As part of the resolution, the Iranians promised to stop helping the Kurds. Because U.S. assistance could get to the Kurds only via Iran, we decided that we could not effectively continue to support that effort; and moreover, our friend and ally the Shah now found it inconvenient for us to do so. So we said to Mr. Barzani and his proud patriots, "Gee, we are sorry; we still love you, but we cannot help you any more." This U.S. step prevented the Israelis from being able to give the Kurds further support. Thus, the Kurdish national revolt collapsed with many thousands of dead citizens.

The Kurdish rebellion was a genuine national movement that we opted to encourage in the beginning, for what I believe were rather, although not entirely, altruistic reasons. Later, because it did not suit our national interests or those of our ally, we cut off the assistance and abandoned the fighters.

That is not the only case of this kind around the world. Do you remember the highlanders in Laos? I could go through quite a list. (I am deliberately not citing the *contra* case, because I think it is different.) What is the moral issue for political leaders in this kind of case? Specifically, what was the moral issue for American leaders?

A third example: Some of us are old enough to remember the Hungarian uprising of 1956. Do you recall the role played by the Voice of America and by many statements made by American leaders, from 1953 to 1956, that we were going to roll back the Iron Curtain, support the cause of freedom in Eastern Europe, and encourage rebellion wherever it could occur? When that rebellion did occur, we looked carefully at the world scene and decided it was not in the interest of either the United States or world peace to risk a major war with the Soviet Union to support the Hungarian rebels. So we did nothing. Of course, the Hungarian regime collapsed, and a lot of people felt guilty.

Now things have turned full circle. The other day in Czechoslovakia, Mr. Dubcek was writing articles. The Czech Spring seems to be coming again, at least something one can talk about in Hungary. Imre Nagy's remains are now being moved to a nicer grave. Evidently, 1956 has not been totally forgotten. These are incidents that weigh on the consciences of a few bureaucrats, politicians, and statesmen who lived through the period; they made choices they did not like but were forced to make. However, they are rarely recalled by the public at large.

In our discussion, the issue of food as a weapon was quite correctly raised. The statement that Richard Joseph quotes from a senior aid official—food aid is essentially political—is totally indefensible; surely there must be something humanitarian about food aid. If its distribution can also serve national interests, I suppose that is not a bad thing. But I am more interested in the morality issue for governments, such as Ethiopia, that do not allow food to go to starving people despite the best efforts of UN, American, and Western donors. Why is it that today's discussion has revolved around only American morality? Aren't political leaders in other countries ever faced with any of these moral choices?

I would like to make a final point about democracy. I think promoting democracy is a good objective for Americans because we believe in it. It is not a matter of selling or merchandising it; rather, it is quite clear that people around the world in every country have the same set of personal needs for human liberty and dignity. On every continent, there is a remarkable desire for democratic institutions, a desire that we have not sold, but that in some sense must have been inspired by the American Revolution.

We need only recall the Chinese students in May 1988, who talked about democracy even though they may not have fully known what it meant. Nonetheless, it served as a powerful concept for them. We should not be ashamed, as Kennan, I think, was ashamed, to say that democracy is a powerful concept.

There is another side to the promotion of democracy, which we have been looking at particularly closely at the United States Institute of Peace. Professor Rudi Rummel, an Institute grantee at the University of Hawaii, has researched extensively and exhaustively and confirmed other academic research about the relationship between the nature of regimes and aggression.

I do not think anyone would argue that democracies do not commit aggression; there are a number of examples, not just American examples, proving the contrary. However, researchers now tell us that there are no real cases in modern times of two democratic regimes going to war against each other, which is an interesting observation. One can go into some theoretical speculation about why that is the case, but the empirical evidence shows that it is so. If this is in fact true, then promoting democratic institutions is also promoting a more peaceful international system, and we need not be ashamed, as Americans, of promoting either.

Richard Joseph: I would like to use this last point to connect with David Little's concluding remarks about the new era into which we hope the world is entering. I think it is important not only to criticize a number of the actions we have discussed today, but also to be able to conceive of a different kind of foreign policy. In other words, the effort to think innovatively must go along with practical action.

The distinction between realists and idealists needs to be questioned. I want to propose a quite different approach, which I think is possible to act on; namely, the practical dimensions of an ethically based foreign policy. We have seen this approach with Noriega in Panama, where the United States expressed a vested interest in having a morally based government in another country.

However, the United States is very selective about the use of this policy; Noriega's was not the only regime involved in drugs and crime and falsifying elections. The arms race in the Third World is very much a consequence of the misapplication of financial resources: the billions of dollars spent on aid are being misused; they are being used in an ideologically determined way. Mr. Mobutu of Zaire is representative, although he is certainly not the only example, of ways in which certain dictators are able to manipulate their patron countries because of ideological ties.

So, because of this policy, we find ourselves supporting regimes that lead to the destruction of education and roads and the creation of debtor nations and dependent peoples through wars and refugees, which we again find ourselves perpetually supporting.

Finally, I would like to make a point about the economic policies of these countries. In some cases, their economic shift from extremely state-centered approaches to pure market approaches is made for ideological reasons, not because of the real economic needs in those countries. In this sense, the kind of realist policy that we have promoted in the past has been very impractical, not only for the countries and the peoples concerned but also for ourselves, because we pay for the arms and the aid, much of which is destroyed before it is of any use.

Afghanistan is another example. After the Soviets withdrew, the United States began to reflect on what had been created. Both countries had fostered many different bands of guerrillas. There were a lot of mines, and many villages were blown up. I read speculations that said, "Now that the Soviets are out, the Afghani government might not be so bad." Try telling that to generations of Afghans, and they will tell about the kinds of conflicts in which they have been involved for years.

Lewis: One thing is certain: The Afghans will eventually have a government that was not made in either Moscow or Washington. I spent more than three years in Afghanistan before the Communists came, and of all the people in the world who will not accept, for any length of time, someone else's version of how they should run their own affairs, Afghans lead the league.

Francis Deng: Let me make a general comment before I respond to an earlier point that I believe was directed to me. Richard alluded to the idea of consistency and credibility in taking positions. I would like to follow up on that. It is true that there are cases, such as the Kurdish case, in which the United States justifies involvement because of commitment to the principle of self-determination. But we must ask whether it acted on principle or simply for the convenience of working with people in order to get at someone else.

The second point on which I agree entirely with Ambassador Lewis is the question of the position of other leaders. The use of food as a weapon is something that I am quite sensitive toward because it has happened in my country; I believe it is a classic case of the need for widening the vision of leadership. What you find in this situation is a crisis of moral leadership; the government perceives the people of the south (who are starving) as directly identified with the rebels—whether they are part of the rebel movement, in the war zone, or have moved to areas held by the government.

The government seems to say to itself—almost explicitly—that as long as the rebels continue the war, they will pay the price in the form of the mass suffering and death of their people. This becomes almost a rational, calculated strategy, aimed at the rebel leaders: you must pay the price for your intransigence by the starvation of your people.

The rebels have their own agenda for war: they believe that all those who deserve to be saved should move to the side of the rebels, into rebel-held areas. Those who decide to stay in the cities held by the government thereby become identified more or less with the government. Therefore, allowing food to go to government-held cities feeds the soldiers and those who are identified as opposing the rebels.

In terms of the moral vacuum, the leaders on both sides have not widened their vision of leadership enough to embrace all the people. This is part of the leadership crisis in a world that is widening its circles but not getting leaders with enough vision to embrace those new circles.

Dayle E. Powell: I would like to build on something that Richard Joseph has pointed out. If we are going to judge U.S. policies, we need to look not only at the amounts of money we spend on arming and fueling these conflicts throughout the world; we also need to compare that amount to the total number of dollars we spend on peace.

One very telling point is with respect to the dues that the United States owes to the UN by virtue of a treaty obligation. We faced a crisis at the UN in December 1988, when the secretary-general was literally asking UN employees to work without salary because the UN was virtually bankrupt.

Had the U.S. government been committed to peace, as it publicly professes to be, I believe it would have been spending dollars on peacemaking and peacekeeping operations, rather than fueling wars throughout the world. The United States seems to take the approach that the world is our chessboard and that the countries throughout the world—and their people—are merely pawns in a larger game.

The ambassador referred to the study being conducted by Rudi Rummel from Hawaii, which indicates that no two democratic regimes are at war with each other, and that this has been the case in modern times. Perhaps one of the reasons for that conclusion is a fundamental premise that underlies why groups are in conflict. It is true not only in the family or community situation, but I believe it is also true in the international situation: parties go to war or become embroiled in conflicts when they feel that their basic needs are not being met. When needs are not being met in the family situation, it leads to fighting, quarreling, and perhaps divorce. When needs are not being met on the national or international level, it can lead to violent conflict or rebellion. For the most part, democratic governments are able to meet the fundamental needs of their populations; thus those citizens do not feel the same degree of frustration felt by citizens who live under more repressive forms of government. I think this is a possible reason, therefore, for the conclusion of Rummel's study.

Lewis: I believe you are right. There are probably some other reasons as well. One is that it is a bit harder for democratic governments to make decisions about aggression because they have to go through a congressional or a parliamentary process; they are open decisions. They also require committing your sons, maybe even your daughters, to wars that are therefore more difficult to undertake.

I would like to return to a point raised by Professor Weber that no one has commented on. He made the assertion that a person holding public office and directing the affairs of a nation has a responsibility—a moral responsibility linked to stewardship, if you will—to the interests of that nation as best that person can define them. He suggested that that responsibility is not synonymous with private morality.

Theodore Weber: The private morality of individuals in conflict is shaped by the morality of their society, which provides protection for them. In international politics, that is not usually the case. However, there are different degrees of moral possibility in international politics, depending on how accepting or hostile the environment is.

Former Lieutenant Colonel North's picture of the world as an evil, Hobbesian world in which everyone is out to get everyone is a view shared by many people and is not something he invented, of course. In that kind of world, you really have to play nasty to survive. But there may also be the pattern that was sketched by a great teacher with whom I had the privilege of studying—Professor Arnold Wolfers— the enmity/amity spectrum.[1]

Wolfers argued that although in the Hobbesian view everyone is at war—latently or overtly—with everyone else, in reality, this is not the case. Some states are hostile toward each other; other states are friendly. The moral possibilities vary depending on the degree of enmity and amity. Furthermore, these relationships are not fixed; they can shift; they can shift dramatically, as is obviously the case with the relationships between the United States and Germany and Japan since World War II. Transformation is possible.

Earlier, I referred to the geopolitical model that so many people thought was fixed in stone—often literally, given the geography. In fact, it is not fixed; it can come apart and shift. The important point, in terms of being able to encourage the moral possibility, is to realize that it is possible to move the relationships of states—at times by leaps, but at least by small degrees—from enmity toward amity. That itself is part of the moral process. Moral responsibility can be exercised in a way that attempts to move states into relationships in which they feel less vulnerable when confronting one another. Whereas they may feel vulnerable when facing other states, they will not feel as vulnerable in these changed relationships. Thus person-to-person and group-to-group relationships vary depending on their substance, degree, scope, and ability to contain conflict.

Wolfers developed this approach partly in reaction to his friend Reinhold Niebuhr, who developed the moral-man-in-immoral-society pattern, which claimed that person-to-person relationships can lead to sacrificial and loving behavior, but group-to-group relating cannot.[2] Wolfers's response to Niebuhr was that he agreed in part, but there were some conditions in which the possibilities for mutuality grew between groups, and we had to look at those. This response convinced Niebuhr and he revised his original typology with its polarity later in his life.[3]

Little: This point about institutional responsibilities is very interesting in light of current experience. It is often argued that the moral responsibility of an officeholder—the president of the United States, for example—is his obligation to or concern for the citizens of his country, which is written into the contract, so to speak, between the citizens and the individual who occupies that office. It would be a mistake, the argument goes, to think of this person as serving only private interests; rather, he is entrusted with a moral responsibility, and the citizens of his country understand that. This understanding is very important, and I think a lack of attention to it sometimes has oversimplified the moral discussion. As fathers or mothers have a special duty to their children when faced with threats or competing interests, so a president might have a similar priority of responsibilities when faced with threats or situations that require making difficult choices.

I would add that the moral dimensions of the president's responsibility have been complicated by recent human rights agreements. Although the United States has not ratified any of these particular agreements (except the genocide treaty), there is the understanding that the president of the United States is in office not simply to serve the moral needs and concerns of the citizens of the United States—although that clearly is a high-priority item—but to balance those concerns with the human rights requirements of other countries with which the United States has dealings. Certainly, Jimmy Carter believed this. Thus, it is no longer a matter of exclusively favoring the United States over the competing opportunities or obligations, but beginning to find ways to define, in a more refined and systematic way, U.S. interests—even moral interests—in relation to the interests of other countries.

I would suggest that the human rights discussion is part of this new global way of thinking that has begun to alter the moral equation so that we—those of us in favor of human rights, at least—now expect our president to incorporate, in an explicit and avowed way, the interests of U.S. citizens balanced by the interests of other nations. The human rights discussion calls for a new enunciation of that kind of calculus and computation.

This leads me to Sam Lewis's list of difficult problem areas. I hesitate to say anything at all because I might end up sounding like a typical moralist who passes judgment on cases he knows nothing about, which is the worst thing a moralist can do. Nevertheless, the point I want to make is that the first step toward a moral analysis of a problem such as the Kurdish, Lebanese, Hungarian, or Ethiopian situations is to account for the entire range of moral questions involved in each case. That is, we would want to hear more than the Kurds' position—the justifications they give and their objectives—we would also want to hear the responses of the relevant governments, their justifications and arguments. Before we could begin to come to a reasonable moral judgment about each case, we would have to take very extensive account of all competing moral claims and counterclaims that would undoubtedly be part of a complex international situation.

I want to stress that this is not a cop-out. On the contrary, this is where moral reflection should begin. My only complaint is that the U.S. government, as far as I can tell, does not seem to engage in this kind of complex, ramified, moral analysis; rather, it continues to talk strictly in terms of interests—and I fear Kennan's influence has contributed to this approach. If you have a theory that rules out morality, it becomes easier to practically exclude it.

Weber: David, I must say once again that you are mis-construing Kennan's position. The insensitivity and the buc-caneering approach you have attributed to him is simply not the way he responds. I would suggest that you consider his comments regarding the British and American plan to take over bases in the Azores during World War II. Kennan was very adamant that they listen closely to the government of Portugal in order to be fully sensitive to the Portuguese considerations, and not simply walk in and take over the islands.[4]

Kennan's personal approach is open to precisely the kind of considerations you talk about; indeed, it demands it.

Little: My point is that he is not always consistent on these matters.

Weber: Then let us recognize that there are cases in which he makes these kind of considerations, and cases in which he does not.

Little: Agreed. Fair play.

Weber: I do not believe we should misconstrue the Kennan approach—which I have heard several people do today. The Kennan approach, for example, would argue that we should not invite people to rebel when we are not going to support them, as, for example, in some of the cases we have discussed today.

Lewis: Let us return again to the questions posed for the president. Lebanon is a very good test case because it is a very difficult case. Administration after administration, despite the fact that there is a large Lebanese-American community in this country, has reached the conclusion that Congress has never disagreed with: while we do have a humanitarian concern for Lebanon, it is not central to our strategic interests in the world. At one point, Reagan did use the word *vital* interest, then he pulled the Marines out about two months later, which shows how vital an interest he really thought it was. Lebanon is clearly not a vital interest; it is not even much of an interest or U.S. governments would have long since responded to the kinds of appeals we have heard from Lebanese.

Yet we watch as thousands of innocent people are killed; we do have power in the eastern Mediterranean, and we could intervene. So what is the moral challenge for the policymaker unless it is, as I was saying a moment ago, that he must live by a different moral standard than private morality?

I am afraid I have a rather depressing thought. I believe, as do several on the panel, that we are now at a real watershed in East-West relations, and it is quite possible, although not inevitable, that the U.S.-Soviet cold war competition will not have the same negative effect in Africa and other Third World countries that it has had in the past.

Let us assume that such will be the case. In the United States, we are also turning inward in many respects and considering with increasing frequency the unmet needs of our own society. Every foreign aid bill has been passed by Congress with the strongly attached argument that aid is a way in which we compete with the Soviets.

I am very afraid that the strife, the ethnic conflict, which will clearly continue in many parts of the world, is going to continue to boil up whether or not we or the Russians meddle in it. The conflicts may be less pernicious without superpower involvement, but to assume that the lack of cold war competition is going to lead to a great burst of American humanitarian sacrifice—financial, economic, and political— for the developing world is, I think, quite unlikely. That reality leads me to conclude, not very optimistically, that the end of the cold war will not necessarily lead to greater peace in many of these regions.

Deng: Something I said earlier leads me to an angle that may not be directly relevant to the immediate conversation, but I think it is important in apportioning responsibility. I am almost backtracking from my original argument about the role of leadership to say that, in a democracy like yours, we know a well-informed foreign ambassador would do well to work hard on Capitol Hill to effect certain policies that may not appeal to the Department of State, and that public opinion in this country can move the government to act in a particular direction or another. The question raised is, Where does the responsibility for action in foreign policy lie?

Similarly, we have seen the effect that the media has had with respect to famine in Africa, or in the current situation in Sudan, when food is used as a weapon. That raises the question of the control of the media: Who directs it?

These circular questions are important in deciding where the moral responsibility for action lies.

Joseph: I would like to respond to that question and present a more optimistic view. About a year ago, I was considering what to do next in my life—one of those small questions. I was spending a lot of time contemplating an invitation from the Carter Center because I had some other very attractive options. I received a call from President Laney of Emory University. This was a turning point in my decision. He talked about the nature of U.S. policy in the world during the modern era—the concerns about geopolitical and national interests. He threw out the name Henry Kissinger—and other people he knew I respected—and suggested that Emory University and the Carter Center might be the focal point for a different kind of U.S. involvement in the world, one that was more internationally based and did not perceive national interests in a very narrow sense. His comments struck a responsive chord with me. Obviously, it is not enough to recognize and declare that we are at a certain moment in history; there is intellectual work to be done.

George Kennan was in for a battering here today; some of it was perhaps unfair, but Kennan reflects his era. He theorized for a particular period, and this is the reason why his argument was so important—not only because it was convincing in itself, but because of the way it expressed the whole issue of containment and the cold war. We are entering a new era, and in many ways we need different Kennans; we need a different kind of base.

With regard to the suggestion that the American people are looking inward, I have seen these swings before. I am part of the sixties generation, and I expect that we will see another swing again, as people grow concerned with being so inward-looking, and students want to look for something more.

In terms of foreign policy, we have to deal with a very practical situation. I was at a conference in Lusaka at which a U.S. aid official made a statement that shocked even the Americans there. He pointed out that U.S. foreign aid to sub-Saharan Africa—one of the largest areas in the world—was only 11 percent of the aid budget, an amount now matched by Italy. Approximately 47 percent goes to Egypt and Israel, and we know why that is the case—security reasons.

The United States and the Soviet Union are not the only ones responsible; the mid-level powers are also players. Even if the United States and the Soviet Union take a more collaborative policy toward particular areas of the world, we have to deal with the Libyas and the Israels, and the role they play in this effort.

So this new moment should be accompanied by new thinking. For example, one thing I would like those of us who deal with Africa to think about is the opportunity for increased cooperation presented by the growing irrelevance of ideology in sub-Saharan Africa. The so-called Communist countries, such as Angola and Mozambique, find themselves looking very desperately for different kinds of economic policies. We are finding that ideological questions are becoming less and less relevant.

Lewis: I want to thank our panel for its very good, creative, and at times disputatious contributions. We have touched on many issues without fully resolving them, but David's paper started us off on a good track. I extend our appreciation again to the Carter Center, Dayle Powell, and President Carter for their hospitality.

Notes

1. Arnold Wolfers, *Discord and Collaboration: Essays on International Politics* (Baltimore: Johns Hopkins University Press, 1962).

2. Reinhold Niebuhr, *Moral Man and Immoral Society* (New York: Scribners, 1932).

3. Reinhold Niebuhr, *Man's Nature and His Communities* (New York: Scribners, 1965).

4. George F. Kennan, *Memoirs, 1925–1950* (Boston: Little, Brown and Co., 1967).

Appendix: "Morality and Foreign Policy"

This article* first appeared in Foreign Affairs, *vol. 64, no. 2 (Winter 1985/86): 205–18.*

In a small volume of lectures published nearly thirty-five years ago,[1] I had the temerity to suggest that the American statesmen of the turn of the twentieth century were unduly legalistic and moralistic in their judgment of the actions of other governments. This seemed to be an approach that carried them away from the sterner requirements of political realism and caused their statements and actions, however impressive to the domestic political audience, to lose effectiveness in the international arena.

These observations were doubtless brought forward too cryptically and thus invited a wide variety of interpretations, not excluding the thesis that I had advocated an amoral, or even immoral, foreign policy for this country. There have since been demands, particularly from the younger generation, that I should make clearer my views on the relationship of moral considerations to American foreign policy. The challenge is a fair one and deserves a response.

---

*Reprinted by permission of Harriet Wasserman Literary Agency, Inc., as agent for the author. Copyright © 1985 by George F. Kennan.

II

Certain distinctions should be made before one wanders farther into this thicket of problems.

First of all, the conduct of diplomacy is the responsibility of governments. For purely practical reasons, this is unavoidable and inalterable. This responsibility is not diminished by the fact that government, in formulating foreign policy, may choose to be influenced by private opinion. What we are talking about, therefore, when we attempt to relate moral considerations to foreign policy, is the behavior of governments, not of individuals or entire peoples.

Second, let us recognize that the functions, commitments and moral obligations of governments are not the same as those of the individual. Government is an agent, not a principal. Its primary obligation is to the *interests* of the national society it represents, not to the moral impulses that individual elements of that society may experience. No more than the attorney vis-à-vis the client, nor the doctor vis-à-vis the patient, can government attempt to insert itself into the consciences of those whose interests it represents.

Let me explain. The interests of the national society for which government has to concern itself are basically those of its military security, the integrity of its political life and the well-being of its people. These needs have no moral quality. They arise from the very existence of the national state in question and from the status of national sovereignty it enjoys. They are the unavoidable necessities of a national existence and therefore not subject to classification as either "good" or "bad." They may be questioned from a detached philosophic point of view. But the government of the sovereign state cannot make such judgments. When it accepts the responsibilities of governing, implicit in that acceptance is the assumption that it is right that the state should be sovereign, that the integrity of its political life should be assured, that its people should enjoy the blessings of military security, material prosperity and a reasonable opportunity for, as the Declaration of Independence put it, the pursuit of happiness. For these assumptions the government needs no moral justification, nor need it accept any moral reproach for acting on the basis of them.

This assertion assumes, however, that the concept of national security taken as the basis for governmental concern is one reasonably, not extravagantly, conceived. In an age of nuclear striking power, national security can never be more than relative; and to the extent that it can be assured at all, it must find its sanction in the intentions of rival powers as well as in their capabilities. A concept of national security that ignores this reality and, above all, one that fails to concede the same legitimacy to the security needs of others that it claims for its own, lays itself open to the same moral reproach from which, in moral circumstances, it would be immune.

Whoever looks thoughtfully at the present situation of the United States in particular will have to agree that to assure these blessings to the American people is a task of such dimensions that the government attempting to meet it successfully will have very little, if any, energy and attention left to devote to other undertakings, including those suggested by the moral impulses of these or those of its citizens.

Finally, let us note that there are no internationally accepted standards of morality to which the U.S. government could appeal if it wished to act in the name of moral principles. It is true that there are certain words and phrases sufficiently high-sounding the world over so that most governments, when asked to declare themselves for or against, will cheerfully subscribe to them, considering that such is their vagueness that the mere act of subscribing to them carries with it no danger of having one's freedom of action significantly impaired. To this category of pronouncements belong such documents as the Kellogg-Briand Pact, the Atlantic Charter, the Yalta Declaration on Liberated Europe, and the prologues of innumerable other international agreements.

Ever since Secretary of State John Hay staged a political coup in 1899 by summoning the supposedly wicked European powers to sign up to the lofty principles of his Open Door notes (principles which neither they nor we had any awkward intention of observing), American statesmen have had a fondness of hurling just such semantic challenges at their foreign counterparts, thereby placing themselves in a graceful posture before domestic American opinion and reaping whatever political fruits are to be derived from the somewhat grudging and embarrassed responses these challenges evoke.

To say these things, I know, is to invite the question: how about the Helsinki accords of 1975? These, of course, were numerous and varied. There is no disposition here to question the value of many of them as refinements of the norms of international intercourse. But there were some, particularly those related to human rights, which it is hard to relegate to any category other than that of the high-minded but innocuous professions just referred to. These accords were declaratory in nature, not contractual. The very general terms in which they were drawn up, involving the use of words and phrases that had different meanings for different people, deprived them of the character of specific obligations to which signatory governments could usefully be held. The Western statesmen who pressed for Soviet adherence to these pronouncements must have been aware that some of them could not be implemented on the Soviet side, within the meanings we would normally attach to their workings, without fundamental changes in the Soviet system of power—changes we had no reason to expect would, or could, be introduced by the men then in power. Whether it is morally commendable to induce others to sign up to declarations, however high-minded in resonance, which one knows will not and cannot be implemented, is a reasonable question. The Western negotiators, in any case, had no reason to plead naïveté as their excuse for doing so.

When we talk about the application of moral standards to foreign policy, therefore, we are not talking about compliance with some clear and generally accepted international code of behavior. If the policies and actions of the U.S. government are to be made to conform to moral standards, those standards are going to have to be America's own, founded on traditional American principles of justice and propriety. When others fail to conform to those principles, and when their failure to conform has an adverse effect on American *interests*, as distinct from political tastes, we have every right to complain and, if necessary, to take retaliatory action. What we cannot do is to assume that our moral standards are theirs as well, and to appeal to those standards as the source of our grievances.

III

So much for basic principles. Let us now consider some categories of action that the U.S. government is frequently asked to take, and sometimes does take, in the name of moral principle.

These actions fall into two broad general categories: those that relate to the behavior of other governments that we find morally unacceptable, and those that relate to the behavior of our own government. Let us take them in that order.

There have been many instances, particularly in recent years, when the U.S. government has taken umbrage at the behavior of other governments on grounds that at least implied moral criteria for judgment, and in some of these instances the verbal protests have been reinforced by more tangible means of pressure. These various interventions have marched, so to speak, under a number of banners: democracy, human rights, majority rule, fidelity to treaties, fidelity to the U.N. Charter, and so on. Their targets have sometimes been the external policies and actions of the offending states, more often the internal practices. The interventions have served, in the eyes of their American inspirers, as demonstrations not only of the moral deficiencies of others but of the positive morality of ourselves; for it was seen as our moral duty to detect these lapses on the part of others, to denounce them before the world, and to assure—as far as we could with measures short of military action—that they were corrected.

Those who have inspired or initiated efforts of this nature would certainly have claimed to be acting in the name of moral principle, and in many instances they would no doubt have been sincere in doing so. But whether the results of this inspiration, like those of so many other good intentions, would justify this claim is questionable from a number of standpoints.

Let us take first those of our interventions that relate to internal practices of the offending governments. Let us reflect for a moment on how these interventions appear in the eyes of the governments in question and of many outsiders.

The situations that arouse our discontent are ones existing, as a rule, far from our own shores. Few of us can profess to be perfect judges of their rights and their wrongs. These are, for the governments in question, matters of internal affairs. It is customary for governments to resent interference by outside powers in affairs of this nature, and if our diplomatic history is any indication, we ourselves are not above resenting and resisting it when we find ourselves its object.

Interventions of this nature can be formally defensible only if the practices against which they are directed are seriously injurious to our interests, rather than just our sensibilities. There will, of course, be those readers who will argue that the encouragement and promotion of democracy elsewhere is always in the interests of the security, political integrity and prosperity of the United States. If this can be demonstrated in a given instance, well and good. But it is not invariably the case. Democracy is a loose term. Many varieties of folly and injustice contrive to masquerade under this designation. The mere fact that a country acquires the trappings of self-government does not automatically mean that the interests of the United States are thereby furthered. There are forms of plebiscitary "democracy" that may well prove less favorable to American interests than a wise and benevolent authoritarianism. There can be tyrannies of a majority as well as tyrannies of a minority, with the one hardly less odious than the other. Hitler came into power (albeit under highly unusual circumstances) with an electoral mandate, and there is scarcely a dictatorship of this age that would not claim the legitimacy of mass support.

There are parts of the world where the main requirement of American security is not an unnatural imitation of the American model but sheer stability, and this last is not always assured by a government of what appears to be popular acclaim. In approaching this question, Americans must overcome their tendency toward generalization and learn to examine each case on its own merits. The best measure of these merits is not the attractiveness of certain general semantic symbols but the effect of the given situation on the tangible and demonstrable interests of the United States.

Furthermore, while we are quick to allege that this or that practice in a foreign country is bad and deserves correction, seldom if ever do we seem to occupy ourselves seriously or realistically with the conceivable alternatives. It seems seldom to occur to us that even if a given situation is bad, the alternatives to it might be worse—even though history provides plenty of examples of just this phenomenon. In the eyes of many Americans it is enough for us to indicate the changes that ought, as we see it, to be made. We assume, of course, that the consequences will be benign and happy ones. But this is not always assured. It is, in any case, not we who are going to have to live with those consequences: it is the offending government and its people. We are demanding, in effect, a species of veto power over those of their practices that we dislike, while denying responsibility for whatever may flow from the acceptance of our demands.

Finally, we might note that our government, in raising such demands, is frequently responding not to its own moral impulses or to any wide general movements of American opinion but rather to pressures generated by politically influential minority elements among us that have some special interest—ethnic, racial, religious, ideological or several of these together—in the foreign situation in question. Sometimes it is the sympathies of these minorities that are most prominently aroused, sometimes their antipathies. But in view of this diversity of motive, the U.S. government, in responding to such pressures and making itself their spokesman, seldom acts consistently. Practices or policies that arouse our official displeasure in one country are cheerfully condoned or ignored in another. What is bad in the behavior of our opponents is good, or at least acceptable, in the case of our friends. What is unobjectionable to us at one period of our history is seen as offensive in another.

This is unfortunate, for a lack of consistency implies a lack of principle in the eyes of much of the world; whereas morality, if not principled, is not really morality. Foreigners, observing these anomalies, may be forgiven for suspecting that what passes as the product of moral inspiration in the rhetoric of our government is more likely to be a fair reflection of the mosaic of residual ethnic loyalties and passions that make themselves felt in the rough and tumble of our political life.

Similar things could be said when it is not the internal practices of the offending government but its actions on the international scene that are at issue. There is, here, the same reluctance to occupy one's self with the conceivable alternatives to the procedures one complains about or with the consequences likely to flow from the acceptance of one's demands. And there is frequently the same lack of consistency in the reaction. The Soviet action in Afghanistan, for example, is condemned, resented and responded to by sanctions. One recalls little of such reaction in the case of the somewhat similar, and apparently no less drastic, action taken by China in Tibet some years ago. The question inevitably arises: is it principle that determines our reaction? Or are there other motives?

Where measures taken by foreign governments affect adversely American interests rather than just American moral sensibilities, protests and retaliation are obviously in order; but then they should be carried forward frankly for what they are, and not allowed to masquerade under the mantle of moral principle.

There will be a tendency, I know, on the part of some readers to see in these observations an apology for the various situations, both domestic and international, against which we have protested and acted in the past. They are not meant to have any such connotations. These words are being written—for whatever this is worth—by one who regards the action in Afghanistan as a grievous and reprehensible mistake of Soviet policy, a mistake that could and should certainly have been avoided. Certain of the procedures of the South African police have been no less odious to me than to many others.

What is being said here does not relate to the reactions of individual Americans, of private organizations in this country, or of the media, to the situations in question. All these may think and say what they like. It relates to the reactions of the U.S. government, as a government among governments, and to the motivation cited for those reactions. Democracy, as Americans understand it, is not necessarily the future of all mankind, nor is it the duty of the U.S. government to assure that it becomes that. Despite frequent assertions to the contrary, not everyone in this world is responsible, after all, for the actions of everyone else, everywhere. Without the power to compel change, there is no responsibility for its absence. In the case of governments it is important for purely practical reasons that the lines of responsibility be kept straight, and that there be, in particular, a clear association of the power to act with the consequences of action or inaction.

IV

If, then, the criticism and reproof of perceived moral lapses in the conduct of others are at best a dubious way of expressing our moral commitment, how about our own policies and actions? Here, at least, the connection between power and responsibility—between the sowing and the reaping—is integral. Can it be true that here, too, there is no room for the application of moral principle and that all must be left to the workings of expediency, national egoism and cynicism?

The answer, of course, is no, but the possibilities that exist are only too often ones that run against the grain of powerful tendencies and reflexes in our political establishment.

In a less than perfect world, where the ideal so obviously lies beyond human reach, it is natural that the avoidance of the worst should often be a more practical undertaking than the achievement of the best, and that some of the strongest imperatives of moral conduct should be ones of a negative rather than a positive nature. The strictures of the Ten Commandments are perhaps the best illustration of this state of affairs. This being the case, it is not surprising that some of the most significant possibilities for the observance of moral considerations in American foreign policy relate to the avoidance of actions that have a negative moral significance, rather than to those from which positive results are to be expected.

Many of these possibilities lie in the intuitive qualities of diplomacy—such things as the methodology, manners, style, restraint and elevation of diplomatic discourse—and they can be illustrated only on the basis of a multitude of minor practical examples, for which this article is not the place. There are, however, two negative considerations that deserve mention here.

The first of these relates to the avoidance of what might be called the histrionics of moralism at the expense of its substance. By that is meant the projection of attitudes, poses and rhetoric that cause us to appear noble and altruistic in the mirror of our own vanity but lack substance when related to the realities of international life. It is a sad feature of the human predicament, in personal as in public life, that whenever one has the agreeable sensation of being impressively moral, one probably is not. What one does without self-consciousness or self-admiration, as a matter of duty or common decency, is apt to be closer to the real thing.

The second of these negative considerations pertains to something commonly called secret operations—a branch of governmental activity closely connected with, but not to be confused with, secret intelligence.

Earlier in this century the great secular despotisms headed by Hitler and Stalin introduced into the pattern of their interaction with other governments' clandestine methods of operation that can only be described as ones of unbridled cynicism, audacity and brutality. These were expressed not only by a total lack of scruple on their own part but also by a boundless contempt for the countries against which these efforts were directed (and, one feels, a certain contempt for themselves as well). This was in essence not new, of course; the relations among the nation-states of earlier centuries abounded in examples of clandestine iniquities of every conceivable variety. But these were usually moderated in practice by a greater underlying sense of humanity and a greater respect for at least the outward decencies of national power. Seldom was their intent so cynically destructive, and never was their scale remotely so great, as some of the efforts we have witnessed in this century.

In recent years these undertakings have been supplemented, in their effects on the Western public, by a wholly different phenomenon arising in a wholly different quarter: namely, the unrestrained personal terrorism that has been employed by certain governments of political movements on the fringes of Europe as well as by radical-criminal elements within Western society itself. These phenomena have represented, at different times, serious challenges to the security of nearly all Western countries. It is not surprising, therefore, that among the reactions evoked has been a demand that fire should be fought with fire, that the countries threatened by efforts of this nature should respond with similar efforts.

No one will deny that resistance to these attacks requires secret intelligence of a superior quality and a severe ruthlessness of punishment wherever they fall afoul of the judicial systems of the countries against which they are directed. It is not intended here to comment in any way on the means by which they might or should be opposed by countries other than the United States. Nor is it intended to suggest that any of these activities that carry into this country should not be met by anything less than the full rigor of the law. On the contrary, one could wish the laws were even more rigorous in this respect. But when it comes to governmental operations—or disguised operations— beyond our borders, we Americans have a problem.

In the years immediately following the Second World War the practices of the Stalin regime in this respect were so far-reaching, and presented so great an apparent danger to a Western Europe still weakened by the vicissitudes of war, that our government felt itself justified in setting up facilities for clandestine defensive operations of its own; all available evidence suggests that it has since conducted a number of activities under this heading. As one of those who, at the time, favored the decision to set up such facilities, I regret today, in light of the experience of the intervening years, that the decision was taken. Operations of this nature are not in character for this country. They do not accord with its traditions or with its established procedures of government. The effort to conduct them involves dilemmas and situations of moral ambiguity in which the American statesman is deprived of principled guidance and loses a sense of what is fitting and what is not. Excessive secrecy, duplicity and clandestine skulduggery are simply not our dish—not only because we are incapable of keeping a secret anyway (our commercial media of communication see to that) but, more importantly, because such operations conflict with our own traditional standards and compromise our diplomacy in other areas.

One must not be dogmatic about such matters, of course. Foreign policy is too intricate a topic to suffer any total taboos. There may be rare moments when a secret operation appears indispensable. A striking example of this was the action of the United States in apprehending the kidnappers of the *Achille Lauro*. But such operations should not be allowed to become a regular and routine feature of the governmental process, cast in the concrete of unquestioned habit and institutionalized bureaucracy. It is there that the dangers lie.

One may say that to deny ourselves this species of capability is to accept a serious limitation on our ability to contend with forces now directed against us. Perhaps; but if so, it is a limitation with which we shall have to live. The success of our diplomacy has always depended, and will continue to depend, on its inherent honesty and openness of purpose and on the forthrightness with which it is carried out. Deprive us of that and we are deprived of our strongest armor and our most effective weapon. If this is a limitation, it is one that reflects no discredit on us. We may accept it in good conscience, for in national as in personal affairs the acceptance of one's limitations is surely one of the first marks of a true morality.

V

So much, then, for the negative imperatives. When we turn to the positive ones there are, again, two that stand out.

The first of them is closely connected with what has just been observed about the acceptance of one's limitations. It relates to the duty of bringing one's commitments and undertakings into a reasonable relationship with one's real possibilities for acting upon the international environment. This is not by any means just a question of military strength, and particularly not of the purely destructive and ultimately self-destructive sort of strength to be found in the nuclear weapon. It is not entirely, or even mainly, a question of foreign policy. It is a duty that requires the shaping of one's society in such a manner that one has maximum control over one's own resources and maximum ability to employ them effectively when there are needs for the advancement of the national interest and the interests of world peace.

A country that has a budgetary deficit and an adverse trade balance both so fantastically high that it is rapidly changing from a major creditor to a major debtor on the world's exchanges, a country whose own enormous internal indebtedness has been permitted to double in less than six years, a country that has permitted its military expenditures to grow so badly out of relationship to the other needs of its economy and so extensively out of reach of political control that the annual spending of hundreds of billions of dollars on "defense" has developed into a national addiction—a country that, in short, has allowed its financial and material affairs to drift into such disorder, is so obviously living beyond its means, and confesses itself unable to live otherwise—is simply not in a position to make the most effective use of its own resources on the international scene, because they are so largely out of its control.

The situation must be understood in relationship to the exorbitant dreams and aspirations of world influence, if not world hegemony—the feeling that we must have the solution to everyone's problems and a finger in every pie—that continue to figure in the assumptions underlying so many American reactions in matters of foreign policy. It must also be understood that in world affairs, as in personal life, example exerts a greater power than precept. A first step along the path of morality would be the frank recognition of the immense gap between what we dream of doing and what we really have to offer, and a resolve, conceived in all humility, to take ourselves under control and to establish a better relationship between our undertakings and our real capabilities.

The second major positive imperative is one that also involves the husbanding and effective use of resources, but it is essentially one of purpose and policy.

Except perhaps in some sectors of American government and opinion, there are few thoughtful people who would not agree that our world is at present faced with two unprecedented and supreme dangers. One is the danger not just of nuclear war but of any major war at all among great industrial powers—an exercise which modern technology has now made suicidal all around. The other is the devastating effect of modern industrialization and overpopulation on the world's natural environment. The one threatens the destruction of civilization through the recklessness and selfishness of its military rivalries, the other through the massive abuse of its natural habitat. Both are relatively new problems, for the solution of which past experience affords little guidance. Both are urgent. The problems of political misgovernment, to which so much of our thinking about moral values has recently related, is as old as the human species itself. It is a problem that will not be solved in our time, and need not be. But the environmental and nuclear crises will brook no delay.

The need for giving priority to the averting of these two overriding dangers has a purely rational basis—a basis in national interest—quite aside from morality. For short of a nuclear war, the worst that our Soviet rivals could do to us, even in our wildest worst-case imaginings, would be a far smaller tragedy than that which would assuredly confront us (and if not us, then our children) if we failed to face up to these two apocalyptic dangers in good time. But is there not also a moral component to this necessity?

Of all the multitudinous celestial bodies of which we have knowledge, our own earth seems to be the only one even remotely so richly endowed with the resources that make possible human life—not only make it possible but surround it with so much natural beauty and healthfulness and magnificence. And to the degree that man has distanced himself from the other animals in such things as self-knowledge, historical awareness and the capacity for creating great beauty (along, alas, with great ugliness), we have to recognize a further mystery, similar to that of the unique endowment of the planet—a mystery that seems to surpass the possibilities of the purely accidental. Is there not, whatever the nature of one's particular God, an element of sacrilege involved in the placing of all this at stake just for the sake of the comforts, the fears and the national rivalries of a single generation? Is there not a moral obligation to recognize in this very uniqueness of the habitat and nature of man the greatest of our moral responsibilities, and to make of ourselves, in our national personification, its guardians and protectors rather than its destroyers?

This, it may be objected, is a religious question, not a moral-political one. True enough, if one will. But the objection invites the further question as to whether there is any such thing as morality that does not rest, consciously or otherwise, on some foundation of religious faith, for the renunciation of self-interest, which is what all morality implies, can never be rationalized by purely secular and materialistic considerations.

VI

The above are only a few random reflections on the great question to which this paper is addressed. But they would seem to suggest, in their entirety, the outlines of an American foreign policy to which moral standards could be more suitably and naturally applied than to that policy which we are conducting today. This would be a policy founded on recognition of the national interest, reasonably conceived, as the legitimate motivation for a large portion of the nation's behavior, and prepared to pursue that interest without either moral pretension or apology. It would be a policy that would seek the possibilities for service to morality primarily in our own behavior, not in our judgment of others. It would restrict our undertakings to the limits established by our own traditions and resources. It would see virtue in our minding our own business wherever there is not some overwhelming reason for minding the business of others. Priority would be given, here, not to the reforming of others but to the averting of the two apocalyptic catastrophes that now hover over the horizons of mankind.

But at the heart of this policy would lie the effort to distinguish at all times between the true substance and the mere appearance of moral behavior. In an age when a number of influences, including the limitations of the electronic media, the widespread substitution of pictorial representation for verbal communication, and the ubiquitous devices of "public relations" and electoral politics, all tend to exalt the image over the essential reality to which that image is taken to relate—in such an age there is a real danger that we may lose altogether our ability to distinguish between the real and the unreal, and, in doing so, lose both the credibility of true moral behavior and the great force such behavior is, admittedly, capable of exerting. To do this would be foolish, unnecessary and self-defeating. There may have been times when the United States could afford such frivolity. This present age, unfortunately, is not one of them.

Note

1. *American Diplomacy 1900–1950* (Chicago: University of Chicago Press, 1951).

Participants in the Public Workshop

Francis Deng is a native of Sudan. Currently a senior fellow at the Brookings Institution, he is also a former Jennings Randolph Distinguished Fellow at the United States Institute of Peace. After receiving his J.S.D. from Yale Law School in 1967, Deng served as a human rights officer in the United Nations Secretariat. He was appointed as Sudan's ambassador to the Scandinavian countries in 1972, to the United States in 1974, and to Canada from 1980 to 1983. Deng served as minister of state for foreign affairs from 1976 to 1980. The author of numerous publications and articles on the Dinka society of Sudan and African development and law, Deng's most recent works include *Seed of Redemption* (1986), *The Search for Peace and Unity in the Sudan* (1987), *The Cry of the Owl* (1989), *Bonds of Silk: The Human Factor in the British Administration of the Sudan* (1989), and *Human Rights in Africa: A Cross-Cultural Perspective* (1990).

Kenneth M. Jensen is director of the Research and Studies Program at the United States Institute of Peace, where he was previously director of the Grants Program. He holds degrees from the University of Colorado, University of Wisconsin, and Moscow State University, USSR. His fields of study include European intellectual history, Russian and Soviet history, history of southeast Europe, history of the Ottoman Empire and its North African possessions, and Russian language and literature. Jensen's doctoral research and subsequent scholarship have focused on Russian Marxist social and political thought. He is the author of *Beyond Marx and Mach: A.A. Bogdanov's*

Filosofiia zhivogo opyta and numerous articles, papers, and reviews in the Russian and Soviet and East European field. He is also consulting editor of *Studies in Soviet Thought* and coeditor (with Fred E. Baumann) of three recently published books on American policy issues: *American Defense Policy and Liberal Democracy; Crime and Punishment: Issues in Criminal Justice;* and *Religion and Politics.* His most recent edited publications produced under the auspices of the United States Institute of Peace include *A Look at "The End of History?",* *Origins of the Cold War: The Novikov, Kennan, and Roberts 'Long Telegrams' of 1946,* and (with W. Scott Thompson, et al.) *Approaches to Peace: An Intellectual Map.*

Richard Joseph is a professor of political science and fellow at the Carter Center of Emory University, where he is the director of the African Governance Program. He has long studied African affairs and has lectured at the University of Khartoum, Sudan; the University of Ibadan, Nigeria; and Dartmouth College. Before he joined the Carter Center, Joseph was a visiting professor at the Kennedy School of Government at Harvard University. In addition, from 1986 to 1988 he was a program officer in the West Africa office of the Ford Foundation, responsible for overseeing human rights, governance, and international affairs. He has written extensively on modern African history and politics, and his most recent work is *Democracy and Prebendal Politics in Nigeria: The Rise and Fall of the Second Republic* (1987).

Samuel W. Lewis became president of the United States Institute of Peace on November 1, 1987, after thirty-one years as a foreign service officer. He retired from the State Department in 1985. In his last post, he was U.S. ambassador to Israel for eight years, first appointed by President Carter and then reaffirmed by President Reagan. He was a prominent actor in Arab-Israeli negotiations, including the Camp David Conference, the Egyptian-Israeli Peace Treaty, and U.S. efforts to bring the Israeli invasion of Lebanon to a peaceful conclusion. He had previously served as assistant secretary of state for international organization affairs, deputy director of the Policy Planning Staff, senior staff member on the National Security Council, a member of the U.S. Agency for International Development mission to Brazil, special assistant to the under secretary of state, and in lengthy assignments to Brazil, Italy, and Afghanistan. Before coming to the Institute, Lewis was diplomat-in-residence at the Johns Hopkins Foreign Policy Institute and a guest scholar at the Brookings Institution. He is a graduate of Yale University (*magna cum laude*), earned an M.A. degree in international relations from the Johns Hopkins University, and also spent a year as a visiting fellow at Princeton University.

David Little is senior scholar in religion, ethics, and human rights at the United States Institute of Peace, where he is director of the Working Group on Religion, Ideology, and Peace, which is conducting a study of intolerance and peace. He was formerly professor of religious studies at the University of Virginia. He was also distinguished visiting professor in humanities at the University of Colorado, and Henry R. Luce Professor in Ethics at Amherst and Haverford colleges, and has taught at Harvard and Yale divinity schools. His areas of specialization are moral philosophy, moral theology, history of ethics, and sociology of religion, with a special focus on comparative ethics, human rights and religious liberty, and ethics and international affairs. Under the auspices of the United States Institute of Peace, he is completing a work that is tentatively titled "Rights and Emergencies: Protecting Human Rights in the Midst of Conflict." His most recent publications include *Ukraine: The Legacy of Intolerance* (1991) and (coauthored with John Kelsay and Abdulaziz Sachedina) *Human Rights and the Conflict of Cultures: Freedom of Religion and Conscience in the West and Islam.*

Dayle E. Powell is fellow and director of the Conflict Resolution Programs at the Carter Center of Emory University. She joined the Center after having served for seven years as assistant U.S. district attorney for the Northern District of Alabama. As a fellow at the Carter Center, Powell has researched international conflicts in Northern Ireland, South Africa, and Cyprus. Working with the Harvard Law School Program on Negotiation, she is currently engaged in the creation of an international negotiation network that will provide neutral third-party assistance to solve both domestic and international conflicts. She is the author of numerous articles and a book, *Legal Approaches to International Negotiations* (forthcoming).

Theodore Weber is a professor of social ethics at the Candler School of Theology, Emory University. An ordained elder of the United Methodist Church, Weber was educated at Louisiana State and Yale Universities. In addition, he has pursued postdoctoral study and taken sabbaticals at the universities of Heidelberg, Munich, and Oxford. He has focused his research on religious ethics, international politics, and war and revolution. Weber has published widely on the subject of morality and politics, including most recently " 'Truth and Political Leadership,' The Presidential Address to the Society of Christian Ethics in the United States and Canada" (*Annual of the Society of Christian Ethics*, 1989) and "Christian Realism, Power, and Peace" (*Theology, Politics, and Peace*, 1989).

Research and Studies Program

To complement its research grants and fellowships for organizations and individuals, the United States Institute of Peace established its own Research and Studies Program in 1988.

Research and Studies projects are designed and directed by the Institute, which supervises their implementation with the assistance of expert consultants and contract researchers. Most projects are carried out through a process that includes the production of working papers on a selected topic and discussion of them by experts in public session. Proceedings from the sessions are redrafted as papers, reports, articles, monographs, and books to assist scholars, educators, journalists, policymakers, and citizens' groups in understanding issues of peace and war.

Research and Studies activities fall into four main categories: study groups, public workshops, working group projects, and studies. Study groups run from four to six months and involve a core group of expert participants in intensive examination of near-term international conflict situations. Public workshops are two- to three-hour events designed for group discussion around a discrete topic of current concern. Working group projects run for one year or longer and proceed through four or more public sessions involving a core group of expert participants. Studies are conceived on the same scale as working groups, but with a changing cast of participants. In all these activities, the Institute strives to provide for representation of a wide range of viewpoints and to address its mandate to contribute to and disseminate knowledge about ways of achieving peace by doing as much work as possible in public session.

Kenneth M. Jensen
Director

Acknowledgments

The editors wish to thank Kimber M. Schraub and David Wurmser for their editorial assistance in preparing the manuscript for this publication. They also wish to express their appreciation to Aileen C. Hefferren for her editorial advice and production assistance, to Joan Engelhardt for production management, and to Marie Marr-Williams for manuscript tracking and cover layout.